Teaching Your Child to Handle Peer Pressure

Linda Friar, Ph.D.,
and Penelope B. Grenoble, Ph.D.

CB

CONTEMPORARY
BOOKS

CHICAGO · NEW YORK

Copyright © 1988 by RGA Publishing Group, Inc.
All rights reserved
Published by Contemporary Books, Inc.
180 North Michigan Avenue, Chicago, Illinois 60601
Manufactured in the United States of America
International Standard Book Number: 0-8092-4671-6

Published simultaneously in Canada by Beaverbooks, Ltd.
195 Allstate Parkway, Valleywood Business Park
Markham, Ontario L3R 4T8 Canada

ACKNOWLEDGMENT

Special thanks to Charlene Solomon, who worked on the original research for this book.

—PBG

CONTENTS

An Introduction to *ParentBooks That Work*

It has been said that twenty-five-dollar words can be used to cover up twenty-five-cent ideas. In our increasingly technological society, jargon and complex language often confuse the meaning of information. This is particularly the case in the social and psychological sciences.

The "hard sciences" such as physics, chemistry, and biology have an advantage: there is little chance, for example, that a photon or a quark will be confused with something else.

In the human sciences, however, we have at least two problems with language. One is that the popular definition of a word such as *sex* or *intelligence* can differ considerably from the way a professional in the field might use it. Although we parents share a common pool of language with social scientists and teachers and therapists, words like *input* and *reinforcement*, *expectations* and *assessment*, mean one thing to parents and another to social science experts. Thus the danger that we will not understand each other is very real.

The human sciences' other language problem is jargon. A particular group of human scientists may develop obscure or seemingly incomprehensible language as a shortcut to communication among its members. Thus, jargon can be a roadblock when the experts try to talk to people outside their field.

The books in this series are the result of skillful collaboration between trained psychologists experienced in family and child development and a seasoned writer. The authors have strived to take twenty-five-dollar ideas and deliver them in language that is clear, concise, and most useful to you. In these six books, the emphasis is on presenting intelligent and practical ideas that you can use to help solve the age-old problems of child rearing.

This brings us to the very reason for these books. It might have occurred to you to ask, "Why should I rely on so-called experts when I can fall back on tradition and conventional wisdom? After all, the human race has survived well on what parents have taught children through the ages." Think about that for a moment. In the long history of human life on this planet, most of our energy has been spent in survival against the elements. It's only in most recent history that we've enjoyed the luxury to live, rather than simply survive. The fact is that the help and advice children need most nowadays has to do with a different level of survival in a world we've created ourselves, a complex world of rapid change.

Even though at moments nature can remind us of her often terrible wrath and power, most of our problems are still manmade. What we—parents and children both—have to learn is to deal with a reality that we have created ourselves.

In the bewildering array of cultures, creeds, and cross-purposes that are modern life, we need a special set of skills to live and be productive. Competition is an essential fact of life. Your child faces stress and pressure from society's expectations from the day he or she is born. To get through, your child needs the best help you can give.

The position of the professional expert is new and revered in our society. The expert is one of our cleverest inventions. Involved in the intense study of one problem or subject, the expert comes to know it better than anyone else. We trust the expert because we know that we don't have the time or ability to sort out everything ourselves. And, if the expert follows the best instincts of his profession, his high level of professional competence will serve you. By using the specialized knowledge of the expert, parents can face the difficult but practical problems of building a family and preparing their children to meet the demands of early childhood and elementary school.

Enlightened by this advice, we can give our children a healthy attitude and a better chance.

These concise and practical books deal with some of the most important issues in young children's lives today. They will help you to help your child and to feel good about your role as a parent. With this in mind, we dedicate this series to you.

Richard H. Thiel, Ph.D.
California State University

INTRODUCTION

Given the many influences that affect our daily lives, it is not unusual for parents to be anxious about their children as they grow up. Many parents are very concerned about their ability to control how their children develop and prepare themselves to face the world.

Although parents tend to worry most about what happens to their children in adolescence, the signs of difficulty can be obvious even in elementary school. Here, even when their children are at a young age, many troubled parents often feel that it's impossible to ignore the handwriting on the wall. Often they explain that they fear that their children will be swayed by their friends in undesirable ways. Children spend more and more time outside of the home, and it becomes more and more difficult for parents to assess and control the influences that may affect their children. A brief scan of a newspaper or a spot check of the nightly TV news provides obvious reasons for the concerns that haunt parents today.

Most of us have seen and heard stories about normal families that have undergone traumatic experiences with children who have run away from home, are in trouble with the law, or in some important way don't behave according to parental and societal expectations. You may wonder if your problems with your own children will blossom into this kind of behavior. You may be frustrated that these problems seem to pop up without warning and in spite of your best efforts to prevent them. These problems you have may be a source of bewilderment and apprehension. Many parents say they feel powerless.

And so it is that parents of young children, even those in elementary school, often speak of fear of early sexual awareness for which children are unprepared and with which they can't cope, as well as experimentation with alcohol and drugs. Although these are indeed serious problems, parents also recite a litany of less dramatic (but nonetheless significant) behavior problems that seem to come from outside the family—such as wearing what parents consider inappropriate dress or hairstyles, hanging around with other children who don't meet with parents' approval, and using slang or overly colloquial language.

If you find yourself in such a position, you should be relieved to know that not only are you not alone in these concerns, but that such outside influences are normal and predictable. There are many factors to which your child is exposed once he leaves the safe haven of the home for school and play. It is your job to be aware and plan ahead so you can prepare your child to cope with the pressures that will befall him. Your child is subject to peer pressure from his first experience with other children, and as a concerned and caring parent, you will find that you will constantly switch in and out of two modes as your child grows: preparing him to cope with potential peer problems and helping him once the problems have occurred. Childhood is not static. Your child may interact constructively with peers at one age and then destructively at another. You can't eliminate peer pressure; it is a fact of your child's life. It is your challenge to be aware of potential problems and to help your child cope.

If problems have occurred because of the influence of peer pressure on your child's behavior, you may be angry and frustrated and quick to attribute the blame for your child's difficulties to the negative influence of his friends. Thus it's not uncommon to hear parents complain, "My son would have been fine, but he got involved with the wrong crowd; I really hate his friends." Or "All the kids are drinking, and I don't know how to help my daughter avoid this." Although it is healthy for you to acknowledge the role that peer pressure can play in a child's life, it is important that you also understand how children can come to be vulnerable to that pressure in the first place. Once this is established, there are strategies you can implement to help your child cope with peer pressure and lead a strong and independent life.

In this book we will first examine the nature and causes of peer pressure, especially as it affects children five through twelve years of age, with some implications for adolescents; then we'll examine some case studies in order to take a look at how it has influenced some individual children and how you can spot it in your child. In the final section, we will present some suggestions for you to help your child avoid undue peer pressure and deal with peer pressure problems once they have occurred. With a little help and planning, you can help your child cope with this predictable and persistent element in his life.

As in all books in this series, we refer to children with male pronouns, such as he or his. Please keep in mind that we are also thinking of your daughter, who faces as much pressure from her peers as her brother does from his.

Part I
The Nature of
Peer Pressure

First let's understand what we're talking about. What exactly *is* peer pressure? Simply put, it is a basic human reaction. It is a need to be related to a social group with which a child is involved. In most cases it's very normal and healthy for children, and adults, to be influenced by their social groups. In fact, conforming to social rules and expectations is necessary and desirable to ensure stability in our individual lives, in our society, and, on a much larger scale, in our civilization. People who find it difficult to at least partially adapt to the group and its values may not be accepted or successful. Most happy, successful people are well accepted in their social groups. There are exceptions, of course; an artist such as Van Gogh, a musician such as Stravinsky, and a writer such as Hemingway are examples of people who did not conform to social rules but nonetheless

3

made significant contributions to our culture. Such individuals, however, are definitely the exception rather than the rule.

As with adults, children's feelings of worth or self-esteem are linked to how well they get along with friends in their age group. One recent study indicates that the most important thing by which children evaluate themselves is how their classmates feel about them. The children were even more concerned about what their friends thought of them than they were about their teachers' attitudes or even their parents'.

Children start to become aware of and concerned about their standing in the group to which they belong in the early elementary grades. It's a normal process. We all define ourselves somewhat by how well we interact with our peers. In fact, if we were to look at it, we adults would sometimes be embarrassed by the lengths we go to to fit into our roles and adhere to the style of our peer groups. From cradle to grave we remain social animals and are influenced by those around us. Both adults and children are engaged in a constant process of copying and learning from the group. We learn skills and absorb socially acceptable action by comparing ourselves with our peers. It helps us to define our various roles and to make sure that we're not *too* different.

Children learn their behavior from adults, including parents, other family members, teachers, coaches, and scout masters. However, they also develop a separate set of skills for sensing what will make them popular with their peers. The peer association is unavoidable (unless you lock your child in his room), and it can be a very valuable, beneficial process in enhancing children's growth and development.

THE POSITIVE SIDE OF PEER PRESSURE

The child's acceptance of the group and his need to be liked by his peers is highly motivating. The child's understanding of the group and the skills he needs to become part of that group will, to varying degrees, affect his later success in life. It is not enough, however, simply to desire to be part of the group and to learn how to behave according to the group's standards; the situation must also flow the other way. The group must show it approves and accepts the child. Individuals able to accomplish this balanced equation will have put in place something that will contribute to their success in life.

An essential part of growing up is learning how to be a human being. In fact (and luckily for both parent and child), most parents realize that at some point their children have to grow up and become independent. If they are very wise, they will also realize that their children's relationships with peers will help them achieve that independence. It may be that in modern society the process of group interaction is accomplished at an earlier age because children are not isolated in the home as much as they were, say, forty years ago. Urban and suburban living, ease of commuting, and exposure to the media all affect the manner in which a child interacts with the world. It would seem very unusual in this day and age for a parent to limit the social experience of a growing child in the ways it might have occurred years ago, when families were isolated from each other and parents depended on the complex of the extended family to help raise children.

THE NEGATIVE SIDE OF PEER PRESSURE

Most parents accept and look forward to their children making friends, enjoying and developing friendships with people outside the home, and adopting values from their social groups. Once children adopt the values of the group, however, and make them part of their own value system, the potential develops for the process to backfire. We all want to be loved and accepted, and it's not unusual for a child who lacks a sense of nurturing and belonging at home to become overly dependent on the security of the group. This child will be more zealous about displaying the correct group behavior and of seeming to act by its values and standards. If the group's values and norms reflect those of the larger society within which it exists—for example, the middle-class values of a small town—there may be little harm in the child's being influenced, even unduly, by his peers. In many ways it may be frustrating for you, who may want something different for your child, but it is part of the process of growing up, and your child will probably experiment with groups and values and roles throughout his early, and even later, years. This will be a challenge for you—and for him.

Most parents will probably identify with this early example of how peer pressure influences children. Your child is beseeching you for a particular toy. You feel the toy is not suitable because it is too aggressive or requires judgment and coordination that your child doesn't possess. Your wisdom, decision, and authority are in control as long as the issue is between the child and you. You have the upper hand. But once the child goes to a friend's house and plays with the toy in question, it becomes a different problem. The toy is popular, and a number of your child's friends already have it (which is why your child wanted it in the first place). Now your child sees that other parents have said OK and he wants one even more. The child comes home and starts to lobby you to buy the toy because "all of my friends have one." You're caught. At that moment you may not realize that you're seeing an example of peer pressure in action, but it will be helpful if you do think of it that way. The way you react to these situations, as insignificant as they may seem, may set the pattern for how you and your child will deal with more important issues in the coming years.

All parents need to develop a kind of built-in sense for determining when to allow their own decisions about their child's behavior to be affected by peer pressure and when to stand their ground. Although an argument about a toy may seem silly, it represents a pattern of interaction between parent and child and may influence how much a child may be swayed by peer pressure later in life.

Another common example is children's clothing. There are few among us who can't remember at least one feud with parents about choice of clothes during childhood or adolescence. It's not uncommon for a child to feel that parents are "straight" and don't want him to dress according to whatever is in fashion. A parent, on the other hand, may feel that the child is asking for clothes that may be too expensive or inappropriate for the child's age. A daughter may want to dress in a more sexual or seductive way than her parents are comfortable with. In the argument that usually follows, the child graphically describes her classmates and what they're wearing. The parents reply with practical explanations for their objections. Often the situation creates bad feelings that aren't resolved.

A third area of concern is the amount of supervision children require. Although all child-parent confrontations are important, issues of toys and dress tend to seem less weighty when compared with decisions involving supervision. The amount of parental supervision a child gets at home or in the homes of others, can relate to the other, more serious problems parents worry about, especially as the child gets older: sexual behavior, alcohol, and drugs.

You may not think that adequate supervision could be an issue with children at the level of the second and third grades. For third-grader Sarah, however, it was. One day Sarah went to her friend Becky's house to play after school, as she often did. On that particular day, however, there was no adult in the home, and the children were "watched" by Becky's seventeen-year-old sister, who, it turned out, spent much of her time entertaining her boyfriend in her bedroom. The two eight-year-olds were left to their own devices. Sarah, who had a good time, told her mother about this, and her mother became very upset. She liked Becky, as Sarah did, and considered her to be a well-behaved and well-mannered child. But Sarah's mother did not accept the type of supervision considered adequate by Becky's family as suitable for the two young girls.

On another occasion Sarah was invited to go to a movie with Becky. Although she felt some misgivings, Sarah's mother allowed her to go with her friend. Again the seventeen-year-old sister was acting in the place of Becky's parents. She picked Sarah up at home and drove the two children to the movies, where she planned to drop them off. Sarah's mother had failed to ask what movie the two girls were going to see, and she was very upset when Sarah told her that Becky's sister had decided on a PG-13 film (one for which parental guidance is suggested for children under thirteen), which contained some explicit sex scenes.

It became obvious to Sarah's mother at this point that she had to begin to set some limits on her daughter's activities with Becky. Sarah's mother had to face the fact that, although her daughter was very fond of Becky and didn't seem to care whether Becky's parents were around, Becky's parents had values that were in conflict with those of Sarah's parents.

The dilemma faced by Sarah's parents is not that uncommon today. All parents want their children to have friends, but changing standards are forcing some parents to rethink whether or not they will allow their children to have friendships with families whose behavioral standards vary significantly from their own. In particular, the standards for supervision of youngsters seem to be changing. More and more children are left in the care of housekeepers, who may not see it as their job, or their responsibility, to set limits on the children in their charge. And so parents are faced with the challenge—and sometimes the conflict—that their child's friends and acquaintances are not supervised. They don't want to keep the child from seeing and visiting friends, but, at the same time, as parents they want to know and be comfortable that when their children are away from home they are safe and not exposed to situations that are potentially dangerous or may cause problems.

PEER PRESSURE: MORE OF A THREAT THAN IT USED TO BE?

Sarah's situation gives rise to a question many parents find themselves wrestling with these days: Is the response to peer pressure more of a threat to our children than it has been in the past? Have the frustrating aspects of peer pressure that parents have always struggled with somehow become more serious when we look at them in the light of modern concerns about adolescent sex, alcohol abuse, and drug dependency? The answer is not simple. Children today are raised in a society of rapid change. The anxiety we all feel when society changes quickly is stronger in children. For many, the answer is to find security in the peer group and to follow its behavior.

Unfortunately, the pressure felt by a child to become part of a group does not exist on an either-or spectrum. It is not as simple as one child saying to another: "If you don't do such and such, none of us will be your friend anymore." It is often far more subtle. Peer pressure is related to a normal desire to be part of the group, which as we said earlier is a predictable human response. For children growing up, giving in to peer pressure provides the security of being a respected member of a group of children of the same age who share similar behavior. This in turn also helps them put together their own system of beliefs, behavior, and values. Thus the influence arising from the need to be part of the group can be very important.

Given this situation, we can see how it can become extremely difficult for children whose parents impose stricter rules on them than their friends are subject to. A common result of this is that children start to feel that their parents are unfair or, worse, untrusting. Most of us can remember the occasions when our parents seemed to have different standards for us than we did for ourselves. It's not much fun to feel that your parents are watching you all the time. Growing up is a process of discovery and of trying one's wings, partially to see where they get clipped. There is a natural tendency for a child to compare the level of supervision outside his own home with what his parents impose on him and to make these comparisons the basis for arguing that his parents don't set normal standards. If the grass is always greener somewhere else, the field may also be larger and there may be fewer fences.

So parents, nowadays especially, are often bombarded with what they see as nagging and unnecessary complaints: "Gee, Mom, most of my friends are allowed to watch whatever they want on cable—they don't even have to ask their parents—but around here, I have to tell you what I want to watch. It's just not fair, Mom!" Mom, of course, has more important things to do than check up on what really goes on at Amy's or Carol's or Richard's. Which means that even if what the child says isn't literally true, other people's standards can be used to "pressure" parents. Or parents may tend to give up restrictions at home as being pointless if their children can experiment with restricted behavior with their friends.

As parents, we hope the important childhood task of achieving independence will take place when our children have enough judgment to be able to avoid trouble and to avoid wrong decisions. Independence should be a gradual process in which children come to be able to encounter outside influences in a constructive way. Many parents' primary concern related to peer pressure, however, is that their child will be influenced by other children or by his social group in a way that may be destructive or unhealthy.

Most parents realize that they won't always be directing or guiding their children in every aspect of their lives and that someday other relationships are going to be more important. Most parents hope, however, that this will be a gradual process—that good friends will become increasingly important as their children get older, but that their children will not "scrub" the values learned at home before they have the wherewithal to replace them with those that are suitable for their own lives.

THE CHANGING ROLE
OF THE FAMILY

As we have said, the need to belong to a group begins as early as elementary school. By first and second grade, children already are beginning to feel the importance of being popular and of being associated with a group of kids who are "with it" socially and know what's going on. This applies less in kindergarten. By first and second grade, however, children start to define who are the popular and successful kids with whom they want to be involved. Actually, by third grade, social arrangements are already quite complex and acutely important to children. There are a number of reasons why this is so and a number of social and economic trends that may have influenced the increased importance of peer acceptance in our children's lives.

One major factor in the lessening of a family's influence on its children is related to changes within the family structure itself. Some of these are obvious, and most have been mentioned in relation to other childhood problems—loss of the extended family, a continuing rise in the divorce rate, and an increase in two-income families, where both parents work outside the home.

1. The Decline of the
Extended Family

Without doubt, this century has surely seen a decline in the influence of the extended family. In the 1940s and 50s, children, when they had grown and finished their education, tended to live and work in the same community in which they were raised. This made it possible for them to have their family relationship with aunts, uncles, grandparents, and cousins—most of whom lived nearby. These relatives felt a particular concern about how children in the family grew up; they may have even played a part in the child's education or marriage. Most important, however, they reinforced the values of the child's parents. This meant that children were raised with a much stronger family influence. For better or worse, they received the attention and concern of a much greater circle of people, people who were involved in their upbringing and who emphasized the beliefs that were the norm of the group to whom their parents belonged.

Additionally, the extended family normally shared the same religion and the same goals. More than that, members of the extended family were dedicated to the welfare of family members, especially the children, and were concerned with how the young people turned out. In short, the extended family provided a sense of community and of caring.

Today, fewer children have the advantage of this kind of large, extended family. Social mobility for job security and advancement is common, and people have literally moved away from their families. Large numbers of children are growing up thousands of miles away from their grandparents, aunts, uncles, and cousins. The importance of being close to our roots has been superseded by the lure of job opportunities and careers, regardless of where they may occur.

The problem is complicated by the number of

women who have entered the work force. Today, when a great number of mothers either want to work or must work, fewer members of the extended family are available for day-care of the child. Thus the child must either fend for himself or be placed in the care of other individuals who may not necessarily share the values and goals and beliefs prevalent in the child's family or that the family would like to instill.

2. The Increase in Divorce

Another important change in the family is the dramatic increase in the divorce rate. Current estimates are that one out of every two marriages ends in divorce, which leaves many children the relics of a broken family. Divorce changes the strength of the family in many ways, especially from the perspective of the child. Divorce is usually very traumatic for adults, and they can be so involved in their own reactions that they sometimes assign less importance to the repercussions of the breakup on the children involved. This is hardly ever an intentional situation, but the effect on the child can thus be doubly traumatic. There are many factors to consider as to how a divorce can influence the needs of a child.

Many divorced parents for a time act like people who have lost control of their lives, who are suffering because something has happened to them that was not what they intended. Studies indicate that most people require from one to three years after divorce to recover from the trauma and to reassemble their lives. The stages that adults endure as a result of divorce are predictable. Common sense suggests that if adults had an understanding of what is likely to happen to them as a result of divorce, they could prepare themselves better, and in the bargain they would be better prepared to help their children.

In the initial stages, for example, both members of the couple are often depressed. One or the other must move to a new location, and both must establish a new household. The question of custody of the children ordinarily becomes critical and depending on how the custody problem is solved, it will have an impact on how the new households will be established. Obviously, routine and daily schedules will change, and one fact that parents often forget, in view of all the changes and pressures they must face, is the ability of their children to cope. Often adults seem to unconsciously think that, because children are "small" and lack the parents' life experience, they do not feel the impact of the divorce in the same way. This may be true. But it is also true that children have their own set of reactions, which too often are not demonstrated outright. Children may not ordinarily say what they're feeling. It would be unusual for a child to say, for example, "Mommy, I'm really upset about the fact that you and Daddy can't agree about finances and have to get a divorce." More likely the child's emotions are likely to surface in behavior, either as tantrums or depression or a medical problem—chronic stomachaches, for example, or headaches. Caught in their own emotional backwater, parents can fail to sense the child's problem and its relationship to the divorce. In fact, lives change to such a degree as a family struggles to come to terms with a divorce that the situation can't help affecting the child.

Typically children of divorced parents will tell a therapist (or anyone else who will listen), "My parents are not at home as much in the evening," or "Nobody eats dinner at the same time anymore," or "My parents don't pay much attention to me anymore; they don't listen to me." Obviously, all divorces are not the same. Even if one of the partners has more or less recovered from the emotional impact of the divorce, he or she may still be in the process of organizing a new household and establishing new social relationships. Divorce often has long-term legal and financial repercussions, all of which may take time to settle.

All of these factors, and the parents' emotional distance from their child, forces the child to come up with his own explanation for his parents' unusual behavior. A child might conclude, for example, that his parents are no longer in control of their own destinies, much less the destiny of their child. This is a disastrous thought for a child to have to deal with, especially a child of today's nuclear family, who may have little emotional and psychological support beyond his parents. *One predictable effect of this type of thinking on the child's part is for him to seek relationships outside his immediate family at a much earlier age than he might have if his family had remained intact.* As much as a parent may grieve for the loss of his or her mate, for the family, for the loss of a way of life, a child must struggle to come to terms with his own sorrow. For him it's also a process complicated by an increased need for emotional and psychological caring, which his parents often are incapable of supplying. It is probably safe to say that to the degree that a parent is less able to meet those needs, the child will attempt to find help elsewhere. It's at this stage that a child often will look to his peer group for the sense of security and belonging that has been disrupted by the breakup of his parents' marriage.

Some experts feel that children of a divorce lose part of their protected, innocent period of childhood. It's extremely difficult for a child even when parents do their best during a divorce. The truth is that it's virtually impossible to separate a child from the problems of divorce—to make everything OK no matter how much effort.

Other things may occur in the course of a divorce. It's not unusual, for example, for a mini parent-child role reversal to take place in which parents actually start to share responsibility with their child and rely on their child as a miniature adult. This deprives the child of that period of protection from adult problems and emotions that he requires for healthy growth and development. Again, often parents are so involved in their own loss and sense of grief that it is difficult for them to see how they are relating to their child. Many adults are completely unprepared for divorce and find themselves at such sixes and sevens emotionally that they are unable to function adequately in a practical sense.

Another fallout from divorce is that the child may now be dividing his time between two households. Shared custody has emerged as a popular concept with the courts in divorce cases, and children are being shuttled back and forth between houses more often than was the case in the past. In this arrangement, both parents may still be caring for the child, but in actuality the child is being exposed to two different routines, two types of rules, and sometimes two different sets of values. During the course of a divorce, the parents are frequently involved in a great deal of conflict related to property settlements, custody, etc., and they may not agree on a whole variety of issues. A child will not only sense the conflict but is likely to be a victim of an inconsistent environment. He may even be forced to make choices (such as which parent he wants to live with) that he doesn't want to make and is unprepared to make.

Any child will experience stress when shifted back and forth between two households. Often, neither parent really knows what's going on with the child at any given time. Ironically, because of the stress that the child is under, peer relationships, which are ideally supposed to only supplement the consistency and security of the home, may turn out to provide the primary continuity and stability in the child's life.

Most parents who opt for joint custody are doing so for positive reasons. They don't want their child to be isolated from one parent or the other, and they want to allow each parent input and access to the child, the idea being that he will benefit from the experience. There are experts, however, including therapists who deal with this problem routinely, who feel that there are benefits of increased stability and decreased stress for the child in traditional divorce/custody arrangements where the child stays in one household during the week and visits the other parent on certain weekends. It might be wise for divorcing parents to ask themselves how it would feel to live in one household on Saturday, Sunday, and Monday and then pick up your belongings and move somewhere else for Tuesday, Wednesday, and Thursday, knowing that Friday night means another move. Faced with such an arrangement, most adults would probably find it impossible to fulfill the obligations of their life—from work to relationships.

And yet we expect children, even young ones, to be able to do so, thinking perhaps that their obligations are not as great as ours. In a child's life this is not true, however. A child must attend school, must be able to succeed in studies, and must maintain relationships with teachers and friends. And he is also faced with the difficult equation of this new situation with his parents. He has more than enough to do without having to carry a toothbrush back and forth between two households.

This is not to say that there aren't children, especially as they get older, who can't adapt to such an arrangement. In the long run, it comes down to individual capabilities. The fact remains, however, that if a child is not comfortable in a joint custody situation, and the parents are not cooperating extremely well, the child might look to his peers for the consistency and security that is missing.

It's the opinion of many therapists that shared custody also allows children to see much more of the conflict that may continue between parents as they strive to recover from their divorce. As children's capacity to deal with situations varies, so does that of their parents. Parents often have not resolved their feelings about each other at the end of the divorce. Experts agree that for parents who are sharing custody, these inevitable conflicts can continue longer and be more apparent to the child. Although the theory behind joint custody is that the divorcing parents will cooperate more in the care and raising of the child, thus hopefully minimizing negative effects on the child that may appear later, many times they're not able to accomplish this. The result is that the child continues to be exposed to parents who simply cannot get together on his behalf.

3. Families with Two Working Parents

Another fundamental change in contemporary family structure is the large increase in families where both parents work. A common result is that child rearing is to a greater or lesser degree the responsibility of non-family members—people who, despite good intentions, aren't necessarily going to be caring for the child in the same way his parents might.

Children whose parents work most likely spend more time with other children in out-of-home care situations. Parents who leave their children in the care of others at an early age find that their lives are complicated because numerous arrangements have to be made for transportation, lunches, and other logistics. Thus a parent may become bogged down with the practical demands of child rearing and have less time or emotional energy left for observing and responding to the child's reactions. And in the large group situations that can often typify day-care, a child will not be supervised—or observed—as closely as he might be at home. Caught between a distracted parent and group supervision in a child-care center, he may learn early on that adults don't have much time to give him the attention he needs. With less direction from adults, he will spend his time with other children, on whom he may come to rely and who may influence him.

Research indicates that early child-care outside the home may not be detrimental, depending on its quality. Parents who both work should carefully observe how their child is responding to the situation and be prepared to make changes. Daily conversation about the child's experiences is important in identifying and dealing with problems early, before more extreme difficulties develop.

THE CHANGES IN SOCIETY

As it has throughout history, the family unit exists within society. Family values and standards of behavior are influenced by those of the larger society, which has its own expectations for the family.

The goals for the family have remained fairly stable throughout the years. Its primary purpose is to provide a safe haven for the child-rearing process and to provide comfort, warmth, and security for family members. Variations of that function have evolved from time to time, and it goes almost without saying that these variations have had effects on the roles and behavior of family members. Recently there have been a number of modifications in society's expectations for the family and in the way it views its members, both children and adults. And these changes have had a direct impact on the increase in our children's reliance on their peer groups.

1. Changing Expectations for Children

Numerous observers have pointed out that today's common attitude about children is to regard them as mini-adults. Children are encouraged to grow up faster these days; they're exposed to more sophisticated information through the media, and because they are often left alone for more of the time, they tend to learn a great deal about life from older friends and their peers (a fear that Sarah's mother was expressing when she decided that it was not acceptable for her daughter to be supervised by a seventeen-year-old).

This is a radical change from, say, thirty years ago when it was still considered essential to protect children from the facts of life. Encouraged by social values, parents felt that children should be shielded from the adult world because they were ill equipped to deal with it. Although most experts agree that there was a little too much protection in that approach, we have tended to allow the pendulum to swing widely in the other direction. Although the intention may be good—that without experience, a child cannot expect to grow and develop the necessary strategies for life. The difficulty may be that we have not spent enough time adequately preparing our children to learn from and use information to which they're exposed. It appears somewhat like the man who had never played tennis but was given a racket and asked to play a tournament game. We assume that children can handle all sorts of information and act appropriately in a variety of situations, which may not be true.

For instance, standards about sexual information have changed dramatically in a generation. Not long ago most children were expected to remain naive about sexual matters until puberty, when there became a "need to know." Even then, many children were never told by an adult about body changes in adolescence, menstruation, masturbation, or conception. Because the media did not show explicit sexual behavior, most children had only the vaguest inklings about human sexuality.

Many parents now believe that this approach was counterproductive and are much more open. Many kindergarten children now know the terms *penis* and *vagina* and have some idea of the sexual act.

The media have also been much more explicit for these new generations. Most children absorb at least some of this information, as well as what their parents tell them. And they certainly respond emotionally, even if they don't quite understand the entire subject. While still in elementary school, children have a smattering of knowledge gleaned from parents, peers, and the media, which makes them sound knowledgeable and adultlike about sexuality. Parents don't seem particularly surprised by this anymore, and it leads to a sense that children are indeed almost "grown up" in this regard. Perhaps parents hope this "sophistication" will help their children negotiate sex and sexual relationships better.

The truth may lie somewhere in between. Children cannot understand the true emotional meaning of all the sexual matters with which they may have become acquainted. And the images in the media have created misimpressions about the emotional aspects and practical side of sex. (For example, few movies or television mention birth control.)

Yet, as a whole, we do seem to expect children to be much wiser about sex. Unfortunately, teenage pregnancy rates don't provide much assurance, and there is not much evidence to suggest that contemporary children are in fact growing up to be better adjusted sexually. *In fact, past research has shown that it is the emotional overtones in which children learn about sex that determines how they will talk about sex as an adult. Knowledge itself is not as important as the feelings about sex that were conveyed along with the information.* And, because children cannot have truly adult feelings about sexuality and sexual relationships, they can only superficially appear adult in their discussions and purported understanding of the complicated issues involved.

2. Children and the Media

Another significant societal development that has had far-reaching effects on children involves the increase in the mass media, increased access to media by children, and a significant change in how television, especially, portrays children. In today's television world children are depicted as all-knowing, often at an early age. Parents are often portrayed as objects of humor to this all-knowing child, who stands off from the situation, watching adults fumble through their adult world. Traditional roles often are reversed, and children are shown providing both practical and emotional advice to adults. It is almost as if TV programming fulfills the wishes of our society—that because we have established the belief that it is desirable for children to face "reality" at an earlier age, they are indeed in possession of the skills to do so. Society today seems to have little time to allow children to remain innocent and protected. Why not expose them to the conflicts of the adult world? That should prepare them to enter it. TV kids are shown to have the skills to do just that, although as parents we may find that these skills are considerably lacking in our own child's life.

Additionally, children are being exposed to adult issues at a much earlier age via TV. In the early days of television certain subjects were carefully monitored. Lucy and Ricky slept in twin beds. Lucy dressed conservatively (if not a bit zanily). The problems of their lives were problems of mistaken identity, misplaced funds, one spouse duping the other for a birthday or anniversary surprise. Today, the problems presented on TV are of a much different nature. The light, comic subjects of years ago have, in many instances, given way to explicit depiction of murder, incest, molestation, and alcohol and drug abuse. Although the programming is basically for adults, many children, especially those who are less supervised, find themselves in front of the television, often with a baby-sitter, watching programs that are unsuitable for them. And although we could argue that the silliness of "I Love Lucy" or "The Honeymooners" was unrelated to the real world, we must also consider the argument that TV is fantasy and that it may be unsuitable for fantasy to be based on the problems of contemporary life.

Through intention or accident, children like Sarah and Becky are also exposed to movies that would have been considered inappropriate a generation ago. The situation is further complicated by increased media access. Children can watch movies on cable TV and on videocassette. Previously, choosing a film for a child was simply a matter of checking the local theater. Today a parent's job is much more difficult because there are so many more "windows" for entertainment available. Cable TV carries R-rated and PG-13 films. TV miniseries frequently deal with subjects unsuitable for young children, and parents may inadvertently bring home videocassettes of films that are inappropriate for their children to view. Thus the media affect children in a variety of ways. While presenting them with false models, independent of adults, the media offers nothing to counteract that image—such as children who are still happily dependent on the protection of their parents and families.

Children have always needed to be accepted by other children their own age. That hasn't changed. What has changed, and what has made parents more alarmed—with good reason—is that the family isn't working in the same powerful way it used to. The family's influence dissipates earlier, and more of our children's needs must be satisfied outside the nuclear family. Combine that with the fact that society—largely through the media—provides an oversupply of information and images of powerful emotional impact, which can shape children's attitudes and values, and the relative role of parents in defining their children's growth seems diminished. Additionally, the media, in a haphazard and often inaccurate way, "inform" children about complicated, often upsetting adult issues that children can only partially grasp and cannot put into proper emotional understanding.

Prepared parents will understand things such as television that influence their child; they will be alert to negative effects of these pressures, and they will be able to take steps to help their child—and themselves—enjoy a happy and nurturing family life.

Remember that growing up is a process. A child who appears capable of dealing with pressure from friends at one age may have difficulties at another. You should be continuously alert for behavior that may result from peer pressure so that you can use your own methods for helping your child cope. Let's take a look at some of the signs you might watch for.

Part II
Identifying
The Signs of
Peer Pressure

Parents have become more and more concerned about the degree of power they have over the behavior of their children. We have seen that much of the negative behavior that distresses parents may be approved by the peer groups with whom their children identify. The desire to belong to a group and adopt that group's standard of behavior is a strong urge in human beings and is essential to the process of growth and development. The difficulty arises when the peer group and the need for acceptance in that group lead your child into trouble—that is, when a child seeking stability and a sense of belonging attempts to obtain it from the peer group instead of from the family, which should be his primary source.

It must be understood, first, that the peer group is

not equipped to take over the role of parent. It has no built-in mechanism for examining and evaluating the suitability or long-term desirability of behavior or values. Where the parent is concerned with the lifelong progress of the child, the peer group may be concerned with the here and now. What's in today may be out tomorrow. What seems so important today may be frowned on in two weeks.

Secondly, the standards of the peer group, as seen by the child, may not match the needs or talents of that child. A child who is struggling with his own development may not be able to become a part of the most successful groups of his peers. If a child doesn't feel that he has the needed social graces to pick and choose peers, he may be attracted to groups in which he feels his acceptance is assured. When lack of skills or confidence leaves a child with fewer social options, he becomes more vulnerable to groups that may be destructive.

Finally, children are perceptive about one another. A needy child may be quickly identified in a group. Recognizing the importance of the necessity to belong and feel wanted, other children may unconsciously push that child, requiring more "far-out" behavior from such an individual. In fact, it is a chicken-and-egg situation. The more desperate a child is for peer acceptance, the further he is likely to be willing to go to gain that acceptance. In turn, the group will recognize this in a child, and, although other, less needy members may not be willing to do extremely outlandish things, they may encourage those who do.

Adults know the experience. Someone who has a

drinking problem may be encouraged to drink by members of a group who are moderating their own alcohol intake. There is a certain enjoyment in seeing someone else in your group getting a little carried away. Adults are, however, usually much more in touch with their limits than children are and can modulate these drives so that they are less likely to get themselves in trouble. Children have not yet developed the appropriate mechanisms for dealing with peer group pressure or with the implications of their actions or the meaningfulness of their limitations.

And so the more desperate child we spoke of becomes the child who can be goaded into driving without a license or experimenting with sex or trying the latest drug. Most children are not so needy that they will allow themselves to be pushed that far, but the truth is that they don't have to be pushed to the extreme in order to suffer the negative effects of feeling too much peer pressure. By giving up their identity to the group, they sacrifice their own growth. They settle for less than they have to, and they may never develop the independence to face life on adult terms. Ironically, this lack of independence may mean that they may not become independent of their parents, or they may adopt such different values and standards of behavior that they will always be at odds with their family's.

Certainly not all difficult childhood and teenage behavior is the result of peer pressure. Life is complicated; growing up in our very demanding society is no easy task, and there are no simple solutions to the problems that children encounter during this process. If, however, you as a parent can understand the need to be accepted, the degree that your child may look to peers for acceptance, you can help him proceed toward a more independent life. Remember that peer pressure is a common part of a "normal" life. The key then is to provide as much security and regularity in your child's life as possible. Then the attraction to be with it, to be in, to be one of the gang will not exert such a great pull that your child eventually is affected adversely. While it is true that as children grow older they need to experiment, to test their limits, to develop their strengths and identify weaknesses, it remains that all children, especially children in the age range of five to twelve, need and desperately want the love and comfort and guidance of a family—no matter what they say and no matter what "squares" they may think you are about hairstyles, clothes, and standards of behavior. Always remember that you are the parent, that you have more wisdom, life experience, and skill, no matter how adult your elementary-aged child may act. Your goal is to help your child benefit from the lessons you've learned.

SPECIFIC INDICATIONS OF A PEER PRESSURE PROBLEM

The following are some specific warning signs that you should be alert to that may show up at various ages between early school years and onto junior high and high school. Each situation directly or indirectly relates to reactions to the peer group as your child sees it and the need to comply.

1. Excessive, intense demands for freedom, privileges, and material things, based on the argument that other children have them. This is a warning sign that you should evaluate your child's view of the peer group and how you've been handling his demands to "be like" the other children.

2. Disregarding your rules in order to do things with other children. This may especially be a problem if you discover this through other channels or if your child is getting in trouble with his friends.

3. Too much concern by your daughter (or, more rarely, your son) about her weight at an early age—talking about dieting and making drastic efforts to lose weight. Be especially alert if you have any indication that your daughter is using laxatives or is inducing vomiting. These signs of anorexia and bulimia are by no means simply a response to a child's insecurity and can become extremely serious.

4. Involvement in competitive sports, but with a lot of anxiety over participating in the activity and concern with failure. Some boys and girls get so anxious over sports that they lose sleep, and adolescents have been driven to the extreme of taking steroids because of a desperate need to be more muscular.

5. Stealing with friends. Although many young children experiment with taking something that doesn't belong to them, your suspicions of frequent stealing by a younger child or any stealing by an older child should not be ignored.

6. Talking about the trouble friends are involved in but denying it for himself. This is a red flag. Children can use this strategy in an attempt to warn their

parents of their own problems. This is a great time for what therapists call active listening, and it is not the time to offer judgments about the quality of your child's friends. (See the companion book *Creating a Good Self-Image in Your Child* for a discussion of active listening.)

7. Any behavior that is willfully destructive to others or others' property done in the company of other children. Like stealing, this behavior, especially in older preadolescent children, demands a strong response by the parent.

8. Indications of sexual activity beyond childhood curiosity or what you feel is appropriate behavior for his age. A child's involvement with sexualized behavior is strongly influenced by his peers.

9. Any hint of alcohol or drug abuse even in young children. If you find any paraphernalia in your house, you may already have a problem. If you catch your child under the influence, you might well assume it's happened before—even if your child says it's the first time. If your child tells you that most of his friends use alcohol or drugs, he may be doing so also. (See the companion volume *How To Be a Good Role Model for Your Child* for further discussion of sex and drug and alcohol abuse.)

10. A discovery that your child has seriously misled you about his friends, whereabouts, or activities. If this happens, you should assume it's not the first time you have not been told the truth. You will need to develop ways to guide and limit your child that include recognizing that your child may be deceiving you some of the time.

These are all signs that your child is having difficulty adjusting to the demands of his peers. If the problem seems severe and your efforts are ineffective, then you might consider seeking some outside help. *Don't wait.* Waiting may only allow the problem to become more severe. An active response to early signs of these more serious problems of growing up often can result in a rapid improvement in your child's and your family's happiness.

ADDITIONAL SIGNS OF A PEER PRESSURE PROBLEM

The following stories are presented to help you understand how peer group pressure works and how it affects children. If you feel that your child is suffering from this problem or that conditions in the home are such that your child may be particularly susceptible, it might be wise to seek professional help. First, however, learn to recognize when it is the group speaking and not just your child. As these case studies show, it's not only one type of child that gets in trouble because of peer pressure; however, some personality traits may suggest that a child is at risk, and some social situations increase that risk.

The Unassertive Child

Unassertive, timid children have more difficulty expressing themselves. They are unable to stand up for themselves with other children and to state and protect their own interests and values. These children will not only have problems in being forceful with their peers but may have difficulty with teachers, parents, and other adults. Parents of such a child may notice that inappropriate behavior frequently occurs in group situations with other children his own or close to his own age.

Therefore, the first question you need to ask as a parent of a child who appears to be timid is: *Is my child assertive enough to be able to say no to friends? Does he have the strength to resist behavior that he feels is wrong or not in his best interest, even if it goes against the majority of his peers?*

Lack of assertiveness can begin at an early age. Many five-year-olds will exhibit signs, especially if they don't know another person very well. In general, this should not be of concern in really young children. However, if you see all these signs in a young child, even in a preschooler, you might want to note that the child may need some help in being assertive as he matures. Certainly by the time a child is six or seven, if he continues to show some of these signs, you should try to help him become comfortable expressing himself.

In assessing your child's capabilities in this area, try to recall instances when your child complained that other children made him do things or when he reported that he "couldn't say no." Think of what your child tells you about how he gets along with friends. Look at it from the viewpoint of your child's ability to be positive. Ask yourself if he has his own plans or activity that he would like to present to his friends. Or does he often not speak up and rarely makes a suggestion when playing with friends?

Some other signs of nonassertive behavior include poor eye contact and the constant use of the expression "I don't know." Often such a child will shrug or say "maybe," when people ask him a direct question about what he might want to do.

Fear of Criticism

Another sign of nonassertiveness is an inability to give or take criticism. Some children have a great deal of difficulty and become extremely upset when criticized for doing something wrong. Actually they may misinterpret what their teachers consider only feedback or the remarks of friends who might simply be expressing some momentary displeasure at something they did. These children also have problems telling others that they don't like something. In issues of friendship, children always will have arguments, and all children are capable of doing things that their friends don't like. Some children, however, are able to give and take criticism, such as "Hey, I don't like it when you take my things" or "You bother me in class," while the timid child will find such remarks very threatening. Sometimes truly unassertive people blow up and lose their tempers, so you must also note whether your child sulks and is unhappy, and then becomes angry and possibly incoherent.

Fear of Not Being Liked

There are other indications of a child who has difficulties with assertiveness. One is an excessive fear of not being liked—a fear that other children aren't going to want to be with him or invite him places or participate in activities with him. All children suffer from this to a degree, but for some children it's extremely painful and something they think about a great deal. Children who try overly hard to please sometimes have problems with their friends, who perceive their lack of assurance. Trying too hard is a sure way not to win any popularity contests. Sometimes in order to avoid conflict, unassertive children will justify or explain away other children's mistreatment.

A big effort to determine what others want and an effort to be pleasing is also a sign of this problem. This can be especially difficult for some parents, because in a sense they find it desirable for children to be that way. Teachers also tend to like children who are pleasing and anticipate what they want. It's a very positive social skill, but it can be very limiting for some children.

Lack of Accountability

Other signs of underassertiveness include being overly apologetic or quick to take the blame for anything that goes wrong, or always complaining of being taken advantage of in friendships. Unassertive children may complain a lot, but when you look more carefully, you will find that they really haven't done anything about the circumstances that disturb them.

Jennifer. Jennifer exemplifies the type of timid child who is most vulnerable to being manipulated by peer pressure and is at high risk of being harmed by its negative effects. Jennifer's experience also demonstrates how difficult it can be for an unassertive child to cope with intense pressure and to confront the expectations of her peers.

Assertiveness in children is relative just as it is among adults. Although most children appear to be relatively unassertive when it comes to dealing with adults, among themselves they may be aggressive about asserting their needs and desires; other children may not be very capable of speaking up about their own feelings and their own rights, while still others may go back and forth between the two, depending upon circumstances. Like adults, children also develop leaders and followers in their environment, which determine who in the group is dominant and who will tend to be more passive and unassertive. And just as adults, children learn to acknowledge this pecking order.

At times, shy and uncertain children will have more difficulty resisting the demands of the group than will more self-confident, independent children. That isn't to say that it always happens that the more timid, less assertive children will necessarily come into more than their share of trouble because of peer group pressure, but that they are vulnerable in certain situations because they don't have the tools to assert themselves.

Such was Jennifer's problem. An attractive ten-year-old, Jennifer was an only child. The family was still intact, and she lived with her parents, who had been very protective and involved with their child. Both parents always regarded Jennifer as being shy and on the quiet side; in fact, they described her as a bit of a worrier.

Throughout her childhood, Jennifer suffered from doubts about her popularity. She often worried about whether people liked her. She was concerned about whether she was bright enough or whether she had the skills to be successful academically. These doubts were not necessarily shared by her teachers, who were always very happy to have her in class. Jennifer was the kind of child they would describe as "no problem." "She's really sweet," one teacher remarked. "She's very sensitive to other people's feelings; she's cooperative, and she tries to please."

Jennifer's mom recalled that one teacher who particularly liked Jennifer had expressed concern that in some ways Jennifer needed to develop more self-confidence. The teacher continued to explain that Jennifer often seemed to have trouble expressing her own ideas and that she expended a great deal of effort to please other people. The teacher observed that Jennifer usually attempted to anticipate what other people wanted to hear from her as opposed to speaking up and expressing her own mind.

Adding to her teacher's observations, Jennifer's mom had also noticed that her daughter would often "come to pieces" in situations when other children would tease her or "give her a hard time." Her mom also remarked that such situations were difficult for her daughter to cope with, and in reaction she often would cry or complain that she didn't want to go to school. Both of her parents suggested that the best thing she could do was to try to stay away from the children who might be giving her trouble. Unfortunately, that advice was all the help they could offer.

Altogether, Jennifer had been raised in what from the outside appeared to be a concerned, loving family. Her parents were responsible, considerate people and had instilled in Jennifer a clear set of values. They attended church regularly, and Jennifer took her religion seriously. The family often talked about the importance of being unselfish, of being a giving and responsible person. In turn, Jennifer's parents felt proud of her as a child whom they thoroughly enjoyed and really had no fundamental concerns about (although her mother did admit that they sometimes wished she was a little more thick-skinned).

In fourth grade Jennifer was befriended by a much more assertive little girl whose name was Joyce. Joyce had no trouble coming up with ideas and speaking her own mind, and in some ways Jennifer's parents were happy to see that their daughter was attracted to this kind of child. They hoped that some of Joyce's assertiveness would rub off on Jennifer. For her part, Jennifer seemed very pleased to have a friend who made it clear that she wanted to play with Jennifer and was active and outgoing.

It was not difficult to see that Jennifer's new friend dominated her. Joyce decided what they were going to do and where they were going to go. As the relationship continued to unfold, Jennifer's parents observed that their daughter regularly gave in to the other child's ideas and style. For a while Jennifer's parents watched the relationship develop but did little to interfere. Although they were not entirely happy about the friendship, they were a bit at a loss about what to do and about its significance in Jennifer's life. Their concern became reality, however, when Jennifer's mother discovered that a piece of her jewelry was missing not long after Joyce had slept overnight at Jennifer's house. Although she suspected Joyce had taken the bracelet, Jennifer's mother had no "evidence" and so assumed there was little she could do about it.

Jennifer and her mother discussed the incident, and Jennifer agreed with her mother that she thought that Joyce had probably taken the jewelry, but neither had any idea of what to do. Jennifer's mother felt uncomfortable with calling Joyce's mom about the theft because she wasn't absolutely certain that Joyce was the culprit. Jennifer's mother also didn't want to upset the family by accusing the child of stealing.

Some weeks went by and the family put the incident aside, although Jennifer's mother made a point of watching Joyce more closely when she was visiting Jennifer. No further stealing was observed, however, and the family felt relieved that this was an unfortunate, isolated incident that, they hoped, wouldn't be repeated.

Late one afternoon, however, Jennifer's mother was shocked to receive a call from the manager of the local convenience store. Jennifer and Joyce had gone to the store to buy some ice cream and had been caught stealing candy bars. Furthermore, the manager told Jennifer's mother that he remembered having seen the girls in the store previously and that they were acting in a suspicious way. Because of this he had resolved to watch them closely—and this time he had caught them red-handed. The manager suggested that Jennifer's mother come up to the store to collect the two girls.

When her mother arrived at the store, Jennifer was terribly upset. She ran to her mother, sobbing and trying to tell her how sorry she was. When her mother asked her how this could have happened, Jennifer could do little more than admit how extremely ashamed she was about what she had done. Her apologies were drowned out by her sobs, and her mother was at a loss to understand what had happened.

Jennifer's mother took the two girls home and called Joyce's mother, who sent the family's baby-sitter to retrieve the child. That evening at dinner Jennifer and her parents talked. Jennifer's mother was beside herself, as was her father. They both felt that they had spent a good deal of time and energy in being attentive to their daughter and reinforcing in her the values of being an obedient child who respected authority. Also, they had always emphasized the importance of honesty and truthfulness. For her part, Jennifer could offer little explanation for what had happened.

The conversation went around and around, with everyone, Jennifer included, becoming more and more upset. After dinner the family continued to discuss the incident. Up until this time Jennifer had been silent, listening to the confusion of her parents. Finally, as things began to calm down, Jennifer was able to explain to them the circumstances that had led her to steal the candy bars. It was fortunate for this family that Jennifer and her parents enjoyed a good relationship and had long before developed what they considered good lines of communication. Jennifer acknowledged to her parents that she and Joyce had stolen on several occasions and that it had made her extremely uncomfortable. Her friend had insisted, however, that she was being silly because "everybody did it." Joyce implied that, although she wanted to continue being friends with Jennifer, this meant that Jennifer would have to go along with her and participate in the stealing. Jennifer had been unable to tell Joyce that she didn't want to steal, and as ashamed and worried as she was about it even before they were caught, she didn't see any way out. She told her parents that she was afraid that if she had an argument with Joyce, she would lose her friendship. In her mind, Jennifer felt that if she told her friend that she wouldn't steal, or if she told her mother about what was happening, Joyce would stop being her friend. Jennifer simply was unable to handle the conflict. Here she had a friend who possessed all the qualities she lacked, who was outgoing and knew how to have fun and wasn't shy about letting her demands be known to others. Joyce was everything that Jennifer was not. And Joyce liked Jennifer and wanted to be her friend. When her friend insisted that the price of the friendship was to do something that Jennifer was not only uncomfortable with but knew was wrong, Jennifer simply had no defenses. She *had* to go along.

Jennifer's parents decided that they would check with Jennifer's teacher to see if she had observed anything unusual about Jennifer's behavior and if she might be able to suggest to them what to do about the situation. Jennifer's mother was very uncomfortable with talking to the teacher about the problem, but it was the only thing both parents could think of to do.

Jennifer's teacher reported that she had observed nothing terribly unusual in Jennifer's behavior recently except that, on occasion, Jennifer seemed somewhat nervous and agitated in class. She also mentioned that Jennifer spent most of her recreation time with Joyce, and this had concerned her somewhat because she had been told by other teachers that Joyce had had some disciplinary problems in the past.

Jennifer's parents were extremely shaken by the incident of Jennifer's stealing and were finally able to tell her teacher about their concerns. The teacher recommended that they might feel relieved by a visit to the family therapist employed by the school system. It took a number of days before Jennifer's parents could make up their mind about seeing the therapist. Finally it was Jennifer's father who insisted that he and his wife call for an appointment.

As a result of their work with the therapist, Jennifer's parents were able to see that in some ways they had not helped Jennifer handle situations like this. The therapist suggested that perhaps it really wasn't the best thing for Jennifer that she be so pliant and timid and as desirous of pleasing as she was, regardless that in many ways these characteristics seemed to endear her to others, for they made her appear to be a problem-free child for parents and teachers.

As the parents talked about it, they realized that they really hadn't provided a model for Jennifer for handling problems. In therapy, Jennifer's mother admitted that she really wasn't much more capable than Jennifer was in dealing with demanding situations. She hadn't been able, for example, to deal with Joyce's mother or with Joyce herself when she thought Joyce had stolen her bracelet.

While her parents' first impulse had been to ground Jennifer and to reemphasize the values of honesty, instead they decided that Jennifer would be more successful if they tried to increase her sense of confidence and give her the courage to set limits within her friendships. Jennifer joined her parents for one of their therapy sessions, and as they listened to her they realized their child wasn't at all sure of herself and that she felt very anxious about having friends. They became convinced that Jennifer didn't lack the values of honesty and respect for property, but they also realized that she did not have the ability to say no to Joyce or other children like her.

Jennifer appreciated her parents' understanding of the theft, and she was encouraged when she realized that her parents' strategy in helping her over the incident was to talk with her about her feelings. Based on her previous relationship with her parents and their expectations of her, Jennifer thought that she would be punished. In fact, she herself thought she was deserving of punishment. Instead of punishing Jennifer, however, her parents came to terms with the fact that part of Jennifer's difficulties related to them. They had allowed her to be shy and rather retiring and had in effect "set her up" for what happened to her. Now their job was to help her be more assertive.

Even after all of this, it was very hard for Jennifer to imagine that she could tell Joyce that she no longer wanted to be her friend or play with her. Joyce called Jennifer on the phone once or twice, but Jennifer always made excuses about having something to do. Despite being angry with Joyce, Jennifer had been taught that it wasn't nice to hurt people's feelings. In fact, it was only after a number of sessions of therapy that Jennifer was finally able to confront Joyce and tell her not only that she could no longer be friends with her but also to explain to her former friend what her own standards of behavior were.

Fortunately, Jennifer's parents supported their daughter's efforts. Her difficulties show, however, that the problems of peer pressure are not solely problems of neglect. In effect, Jennifer's parents had shielded her from experience. They felt, as many parents believed many years ago, that it was best to protect their child from the harsher realities of life. The family actually admitted that this strategy was a kind of backlash to the permissiveness they saw around them. In order to protect Jennifer they had hidden her from the challenges and conflicts of life. The result was that she couldn't cope when she was faced with a friend like Joyce. While the lessons of contemporary society seem to point to the demanding person as the one who will get ahead, Jennifer's parents were trying to teach her that the way to succeed is to steer clear of making demands on people.

The Impulsive Child

At the other end of the spectrum is the impulsive child. These children often get into trouble because they're looking for excitement. They usually are carried away with the group and lack the skills to think through the consequences of what they're going to do. Almost all young children are impulsive, which is why they need a great deal of supervision and adults can't count on them to exercise self-control and restraint. Although by first grade children are expected to sit, follow instructions, and take some responsibility, nonetheless even at this age some children continue to be highly impulsive. Obviously, not all children mature at the same rate, and it's more common to see boys behaving this way, but girls are known to also.

Failure to Understand Cause and Effect

Often the mistakes that these children make or the trouble they get into are not premeditated—they just "happen." At least that's how it seems to the child. He may not appear to be in a bad mood or looking for trouble—but "one thing led to another," and there he was.

Impulsive children are often quickly bored and frustrated. They tend to have less emotional control than the average child. Children such as this are often described as "just not thinking" or "lacking common sense." Parents complain, "I'm always telling him to slow down. He gets so wound up, he drives me crazy." When parents characterize an impulsive child, they often talk about him in terms that seem to fit much younger children. Other complaints parents voice include a failure to stick with anything: "Nothing ever gets finished; he's always dashing off to something else."

Desire for Confusion and Tumult

It is not unusual for many children to be unable to control certain impulses; such children are easily excitable, and as often as not they relish exhilaration and tumult. Highly impulsive children, however, are overly susceptible to getting into trouble with friends—first, because they're genuinely attracted to circumstances that promise intense stimulation and, second, because they seem to be more excitable in group situations.

These children are described by pat phrases like "throwing caution to the wind," "not looking before they leap," or "full of the devil." Teachers are very familiar with these types of children, whom therapists sometimes describe as "acting out" their feelings of excitement and intensity and who are inspired by other children who act out their emotions.

Teachers are all too accustomed to the situation in which one child inspires or attracts a cluster of likeminded children, who then feed off each other and manage to get into difficulty.

The behavior that such children display can be negative and potentially destructive. They might band together on a freeway overpass, for example, and throw rocks at passing cars. On a hike in the country they would be the scouts who ignore the "No Trespassing" or "Danger" signs. If asked why, they would tell you, "Because it's exciting."

Attraction to this kind of peer group, of course, detracts from, rather than encourages, good judgment. Instead of thinking about what they want to do, a group of excited youngsters may do things that none of the children would do if they were alone.

Both children and adults tend to become more excited in group and social situations, and children who are already excitable and impulsive tend to display their worst judgment in social situations with other children who are also overly excitable. Their natural tendencies are reinforced by the group.

Eric. We discussed in the first section of this book the changes that have taken place in our social attitudes and values, including the slackening of supervision for young children. The case of eight-year-old Eric illustrates how these changes can interact with a child's personality in a way that leads to problems. Eric is a typical example of a vulnerable child who is susceptible to getting into trouble with friends. He is a child who seems to be in constant difficulty because he's impulsive and is engaged in a constant search for stimulation.

The younger of two children, Eric has an older brother named Jason who has a much quieter personality than Eric. The boys' parents were divorced when Eric was two, and both of the boys see their father relatively infrequently. This apparently bothers Eric more than Jason.

Eric's mother describes him as a child who never sits still—"a perpetual motion machine." She describes him as likable but says that on certain occasions he can become "uncontrollable."

When Eric was ready for first grade, his mother thought that he was not growing up as fast as his classmates and decided to keep him in kindergarten, hoping that he would grow out of some of his excitability. As a student, Eric was a bit below the class average but was clearly capable of achieving passing grades. His teacher said he was brighter than his marks showed but that his performance suffered because he was easily distracted and overactive in the classroom. If, for example, another child was acting silly, Eric's attention was immediately diverted from his work and he would often begin to act up himself. If nothing was happening, he frequently chose to provide the excitement for the others. He was one of those boys who made funny noises in class to distract the other children. Even when he was in third grade, he would pull such stunts as falling over on his chair fairly often—he would lean backward, lose concentration, and fall over.

In the absence of his father, whom he missed terribly, Eric adored his older brother and tried desperately to imitate him. He took up the same sports his brother was involved in and even imitated his brother's swagger and style. By third grade, Eric's bluster and attention-getting antics had made him popular with the other boys. The girls in his class, however, tended to think that he was a nuisance because he teased them and played in a rough manner.

As might have been predicted, Eric's form of misbehavior was often spur-of-the-moment pranks. By the time he was in fourth grade, he had been involved in a number of minor escapades. At a Cub Scout meeting one night in December he and a friend sneaked into an adjacent room of the church hall where the meeting was held. While the rest of the scouts were being quizzed about trees they would see on a hike the following Sunday, Eric and his friend ate the plate of cookies that had been set out for the Ladies' Book Review Club scheduled to meet after the Scouts had left.

On another occasion Eric and two friends—although they had been distinctly forbidden to do so—rode their bicycles across town and through several busy intersections to an arcade, where they each spent several dollars on video games. The money they used to play the machines had been stolen by one of the older boys from his mother's purse.

On one hand, Eric's mother was glad that the child had a lot of friends. It helped keep him busy while she was at work. She was a single working parent and received very little help from Eric's father, who was erratic in his child-care payments and visited the family infrequently, although the boys often complained to their mother that they missed their dad and wanted to spend more time with him. Because he was well liked and had a number of friends, Eric was not the kind of child who spent hours by himself in the family's apartment. Instead he was in the habit of taking long rides on his bike after school, often ending up at a friend's house. Then the two would collect a few of their other friends and the whole group would amuse themselves with various games and escapades until it was time for everyone to go home for dinner.

It's not surprising that Eric's mother considered this arrangement a mixed blessing. Although she was happy that Eric was able to be relatively self-sufficient in entertaining himself at an early age, she also knew that her son had not yet developed a sound sense of judgment. At one time, being aware of his temperament, she had attempted to place Eric in after-school care. However, he complained that the time he spent there was boring, so his mother finally gave up and allowed him to fend for himself. Her decision was also partially a monetary one. If Eric was not enjoying himself in costly after-school care and seemed to be able to take care of himself until she returned from work, there were a number of other things she could use the money for.

Eric had one special friend whose home he visited frequently after school. Sometimes he would have dinner there and come home around seven, when he would do his homework and his mom would get him ready for bed. Because she had no reason to think otherwise, Eric's mother presumed that the boys were being supervised by the other child's parent. She knew that the boys rode around on their bikes in the neighborhood and that sometimes they would go back to the schoolyard to play. Distracted by her money problems and attempts to juggle her time so that she could be with the boys and still have a few moments left over for herself, she allowed Eric to join his friends on their bikes as long as their eventual destination was the schoolyard.

One evening after school Eric and a couple of his friends rode their bikes to the school as usual. There they met three older boys from school, one of whom had provided the stolen money for the video games. The older boys had brought a can of spray paint. It didn't take very long for the group to determine what they wanted to do with the paint. Each took turns at the can, and when they had finished, all the walls that bordered the play yard were covered with graffiti. Excited by the activity and not to be outdone, Eric had grabbed the can of spray paint and painted a streak of black across the hood of a silver sports car parked in the nearby teachers' lot. The boys, who were all very excited and laughing, urged Eric on and applauded his efforts. All of them knew that what they were doing was wrong, but in the excitement of the moment none of them had thought of the possible consequences if they were caught.

After a while the group broke up and Eric went home. He quickly slipped by his mother and went directly to his room, telling his mother that he was going to do his homework. She would remember later that he acted almost as though he wanted to avoid seeing her. Although he may not consciously have known what he was doing, Eric was attempting to avoid his mother's questions in case somehow she had heard what had happened in the playground.

As it turned out, a neighbor had seen the boys spray-painting and was able to identify one of the older children to the police. Officers investigated, and soon the police had the names of all the children involved. Eric's mother was completely taken aback the next day when an officer called her at work and told her of Eric's part in the graffiti spree. Because older boys were involved and Eric's younger friends seemed very distressed and contrite about what they had done, the boys were let off with just a severe warning. For Eric (and his mother), the price was higher. Under pressure from the police, one of the older boys identified Eric as the culprit who had spray-painted the math teacher's car, and Eric's family was forced to pay for the cost of repainting the automobile.

Much to his mother's despair, the incident also served to increase Eric's reputation at school as troublemaker. Although he knew his behavior had upset his mother terribly, Eric was caught in a conflict, because some of the children at school thought he had been very daring and had managed "to get away with it." It was as though Eric felt flattered, even though he knew he had done something very wrong.

Upset by his behavior and the price she had to pay for it, Eric's mother grounded him for three weeks, which meant that he had to go directly home after school and stay in the apartment. Because she worked, Eric's mother asked Jason to monitor Eric; Jason was supposed to report to her if Eric disobeyed the rule to return home immediately after school. Jason voiced his complaints about the job, however, referring to himself as a watchdog and telling his mother that it was unfair to both boys. Nonetheless, his mother prevailed, and Jason agreed to check on Eric as long as his responsibility lasted for only three weeks.

During his "probation" period, Eric acted very contrite and cooperative. He and his mother had several long talks about respecting other people's property, and, as a result, she decided to allow Eric to return to his former arrangement, except that she would no longer agree to his staying late at his friends' houses. She insisted that the boy be home for dinner each night.

Although she did not see many choices available to her, by deciding to return to their previous arrangement Eric's mother was simply buying time before Eric would find some other situation in which he would get into trouble again. It was really not enough to ask Eric to be home for dinner. What Eric's mother had failed to recognize was that Eric was suffering considerably from the loss of his dad and the disruption of his home environment. In such situations, the problem has become so acute that professional help is advised.

Although he is by nature excitable and high-spirited, these characteristics may not have been as much of a problem for Eric if he had had proper outlets for his energy. He remembers hunting and fishing trips with his father and a game of wrestling they used to play. Part of his distracting behavior at school results from a need to test himself physically, as he was able to do with his father. Eric's brother has not suffered as much because he is a more curious child and would rather spend time on school projects and in supervised activity at school. The boys' mother, who had studied to be a history teacher and was forced to forsake her schooling when her husband abandoned the family, identifies more closely with Jason than she does with Eric. Thus, helping Jason with his schoolwork fulfills a need in her, and she spends more time with her older son than with Eric.

Eric needs much more structure and supervision in his life—and probably some professional therapy to help him and his family overcome the loss of his father and the feelings of insecurity that arise from living in a one-parent home. A therapist might be able to help him become more independent—to build his own identity in a positive way rather than in a way that will continue to target him as a problem.

The Child Who Feels Socially Disadvantaged

Children can feel disadvantaged within their peer groups because of handicaps that they think they see in themselves or that may be related to their family situations. These handicaps aren't necessarily *real*, but they are perceived that way by the child. The most common symptoms are that the child doesn't feel that he measures up economically or academically to the standards of his peer group. Such children are inhibited, feel needy, and less independent. We often speak of them as feeling "one down," and they typically feel very bad when they can't comply with the group. These are children we see working the hardest to dress the right way, do the right things, and acquire the right possessions.

Feelings of Being Disadvantaged

Children who feel disadvantaged by the standards of their peers are generally much more vulnerable to group pressure. For example, a *moderately* wealthy child in a *very* wealthy community may feel disadvantaged. To the child this may be a matter of family finances, or social status or background that "doesn't measure up." Other children may feel they aren't physically attractive or that their talents are inferior. The result is that they often develop into "experts" at justifying their feelings of being at a disadvantage. Often these children attempt to over-compensate because of their great need to be like everyone else. They are highly motivated in their attempts to meet—and perhaps exceed—what they see as the group standards. These children routinely suffer from a reduced sense of self-esteem.

Sometimes parents who feel that they, or their child, are at a disadvantage will themselves fuel the child's feeling and make extra efforts to provide for the child. The parents' own anxieties add to the child's. As a result, the child learns at a very early age to be demanding and dissatisfied.

It is not at all unusual for children from modest backgrounds who attend prestigious private schools to feel ill at ease. They focus their attention on the most affluent children in the school and use them as their standards. They develop strong needs to asso-ciate with and be like the other children. Those chil-dren who see themselves as not having the things other children have often have a greater need to strive to be part of that group—and are willing to do more to become a group member, to engage in more outlandish behavior than the other children, and to take greater risks of offending their parents and other authority figures.

This is not to say that children can't benefit from their differences or that they do well only associat-ing with a group of children very much like them-selves. Part of being an independent adult is the ability to maintain confidence regardless of circum-stances. In developing a sense of confidence, how-ever, most children need to feel accepted and respected by their peers even if they are not exactly like the group in every way.

A child may feel accepted in a variety of ways. Special talents, a winning personality, a good self-concept fostered by the family, participation in school activities, and good social skills all contribute to a child's feeling good about himself. Furthermore, some children seem to need more acceptance than others. Feeling socially disadvantaged in a group comes from an interaction of the peer group itself and the child's sense of self. One child may have only one or two friends and not be considered particularly popular and yet be content and confident. Another child with similar social success may see his social life as a failure and feel self-conscious and upset that he isn't more popular.

Parents have the possibility to help a child before he begins to feel disadvantaged. Some of the factors you might consider are:

1. Where does your child fit into his peer group in terms of academic ability, finances, physical agility? Are there liable to be problems because he differs from his peers in very important ways?

2. What are the group's values? For example, does the school put a high priority on athletics when your child is relatively weak in that area?

3. Is your child different in race, religion, cultural background from his real or potential peer group? As stated previously, differences can be helpful. Much will depend on how your child and his friends see these differences and the degree of confidence your child has in being accepted.

After you've answered these questions, and if there are many differences between your child's background and abilities and those of the children in his peer group, then you should take the time to discuss with your child how he can feel better about himself and make more friends. You should attempt to help him feel a sense of self-worth and explain that he will be liked for what/who he is and that differences are not necessarily all that important. And then watch carefully for signs that your child is becoming upset about his relationships with his peers.

As discussed in Part One, another reason that children often show undesirable behavior as a result of peer pressure can be that they see their families as rejecting them or having failed in some way. For that reason they have a greater need to identify with and please their friends. They look to their peers for acceptance and to fulfill the need for love and nurturing they have not had in their family.

We have suggested a number of factors that can cause such children to feel socially disadvantaged or different from the rest of their peer group—their family's finances or social position, their own level of accomplishments, physical attractiveness, success in extracurricular school activities, constant harassment at home about their capabilities, or the failure of family and teachers to provide opportunities for them to show what they can do. If such children feel different and disadvantaged in some way, they will easily bow to the pressures of the group and have more trouble being independent. This problem can become more severe as a child grows older; take the case of Kevin and Susan, for example.

Kevin and Susan. Kevin and Susan are two siblings whose parents dragged the family through a bitter divorce, which exposed the children to arguments and tensions that disturbed the entire household and frustrated the children. Kevin and Susan also suffered in the aftermath of the divorce when their mother, in particular, became depressed and unable to maintain an organized household. Both children were ordered by the court to live with their mother, although Kevin would have preferred to be with his father. The father was a high-level movie company executive, however, and traveled at least two weeks out of the month, and the court ruled that Kevin's well-being would be in jeopardy if he were to live in such a transient household. His father did not contest the court decision, and this caused feelings of desertion and abandonment in the boy.

Because Kevin's preference for living with his father was denied and because their mother did not seem to care about establishing a stable home for the family, the children were left with the feeling that neither parent really cared about them and that the parents were so preoccupied with their own problems in the time immediately after the divorce that they actually neglected the children.

Both parents were competitive and materialistic. The father had slowly risen through the ranks of the business affairs departments of a number of studios, and the mother was a well-known screenwriter. Encouraged by their parents to compete, and given the means to do so, Kevin and Susan proceeded full speed ahead. Kevin was the first-string quarterback on the high school football team and the captain of the school's award-winning debate team. His sister was a senior who had already won early acceptance to a local university and would go on to study physics the next June when she graduated from high school.

Despite the fact of their own success and relative affluence, however, Kevin and Susan's parents had a compulsion to be thrifty. Money was a very important issue within the family. At the time of the divorce, this caused a great deal of confusion in the children, who had been urged to compete and had both achieved positions in the most affluent clique in the school. This had put considerable demands on the children to dress well, to have relatively large amounts of spending money, and to be generally up on what was in.

When their parents divorced, Kevin and Susan heard both sides of their parents' arguments about who was at fault, and they suffered through the threat made by both parents that the family would have to lower its standard of living. Each parent felt cheated and deprived as a result of the failure of the marriage—although both had been so distracted by their careers that they had actually devoted a small amount of their time and energy to making the marriage work. The divorce settlement required selling the family home and dividing the profits so that each parent could establish a separate residence. The children's father bought a very modern condominium in Beverly Hills and their mother a small, older home on the outskirts of adjacent Century City.

The bitterness that followed the divorce took the form of frequent outbursts toward the children. There was a great deal of talk that the family would no longer be able to enjoy their annual extended vacations and bitter jokes about how the children would soon have to shop at low-cost discount stores instead of the trendy boutiques they were used to. Each parent found it extremely difficult not to blame the other for the situation.

The parents' anger at each other began to dominate the children's lives. Both children began to show signs of the strain, to the point that Kevin's teacher began to notice his tenseness and anxiety in class. Both children were troubled and distressed about what they saw as an insecure future, and considering their standing in the school community, they felt a great sense of shame about what had happened to their family.

Despite all their disagreements, the parents did concede that the children should continue to attend the private school in which they were enrolled at the time of the divorce, although they had considerable discussions about who was going to pay the tuition and the various other expenses involved. Each quarter, as the tuition bill came due, there would be renewed tension about how it was to be paid, specifically whether it should come out of the parents' pockets or be deducted from other miscellaneous child-care costs. The children were aware of these discussions and felt very self-conscious about the difficulties they saw that they were causing. In their eyes, they were causing the continuation of hostilities between their parents.

The school that the two children attended was chosen not only for its reputation for academic excellence but also because of its high social status.

Thus, in the face of having to "keep up appearances" with the other children, it was doubly difficult for the two children to deal with the problems caused by their parents' divorce. Both Kevin and Susan began to feel somewhat like outcasts in their school group. First, they were from a divorced family, which, although not uncommon in that school, they were having difficulty adjusting to; and second, they felt like they were the only children in the school whose parents were concerned about money. When they brought friends home, it was to a new, smaller house—especially small compared to the homes of some of their classmates. And, because the parents' joint custody arrangement meant alternating weekends and dividing the week between the two homes, the children often found themselves at their father's condo (which was farther away from their school) when they wanted to be near the school to attend an event or be with their friends.

Each parent had a housekeeper, and because each was attempting to reconstruct a social life, the children more often found themselves with the hired help than with either of their parents. This was particularly true with their dad, who frequently had business in the East and always seemed to be jetting off to New York or Boston or someplace the children had never been (although on one of the extended vacations the family had taken a three-week trip to Europe). The entire situation was becoming more confusing and distressing for the two children. The arguments about tuition continued, and the fear of having to attend public school hovered constantly over both households. To both Kevin and Susan, public school would have been the clearest indication of their parents' failure to maintain their former standard of living, on which they had based their competitive desires for their children. Public school represented to the children the proof that their family had failed—that their parents were not going to be able to provide for them in important ways.

Both children also became increasingly concerned about clothes, insisting that they continue to shop in their usual stores and becoming even more compulsive about having the latest styles.

Neither parent seemed to understand how desperately their children needed to receive approval and be accepted by their friends. Given all the other disturbances they had gone through, it was even more important that they be accepted and popular in their school. They felt that, by having the right clothes and car and other material goodies, they would remain in good standing with their peer group. They didn't want to seem different. During the summer Susan pleaded that she be sent to an extremely expensive horse camp. She listed all the other girls in the school who were going. At first her parents refused, citing the expense. Susan retaliated by becoming distressed and angry and withdrew from the family. Her parents finally gave up and offered to send her for part of the session.

As they slowly recovered from their own confusion and depression as a result of the divorce, Kevin and Susan's parents each attempted to set aside time to spend with the children. They discovered, however, that neither child expressed much interest in being with them anymore and in fact became hostile and nervous in their presence. The children had substituted their own activities during the time that they had usually spent with their parents and now preferred these activities.

The parents did notice, however, that both children appeared depressed and moody. One teacher remarked that although the children were doing well and had close friends, they seemed to be extremely pressured. The teacher indicated her concern that neither child was willing to talk to any of the school's staff about their problems, but instead they were expending a great amount of energy attempting to excel in a variety of school activities.

Upset by her own reactions to the divorce and concerned about the lack of direction in her own life, the children's mother decided to enter therapy. She was genuinely concerned about a number of failures in her writing that had surfaced not long after the divorce had become final and she had moved into her new home. Since not only her financial but her artistic existence depended on being able to write, she was extremely motivated in therapy and did well in a short period of time. Enthused by her success and encouraged by the therapist, she decided to include the children in one or two of the sessions. The initial talks with the two children were relatively disappointing and unsuccessful. During the third visit, however, the children began to open up. They spoke about their sense of abandonment and their anger about what they saw as their parents' hypocrisy regarding money.

As difficult as it was for her to do so, Kevin and Susan's mother was able to listen to her children. Slowly she began to realize what had happened to the children, and with the therapist's help the broken family began to feel better about each other. In particular, Kevin and Susan's mother began to get in touch with her feelings about the children that had been sublimated during the divorce and its aftermath. Slowly she began to understand what the children had gone through in the separation from their father and the neglect they felt.

As a result of understanding some of the underlying causes of her children's problems, Kevin and Susan's mother was able to get rid of the anger she had felt toward the children, their school, and what she saw as the children's increasing snobbishness and materialism. She realized the difficulties the children were undergoing, and she was able to admit that in large part they had been caused by the broken family situation. Although the family has a long road ahead of it, mother and children at least have taken the right step in identifying the source of their problems and agreeing to work together to solve them.

If you recognize common denominators in your child's behavior and the children described in these three profiles, especially if your child is in the lower elementary grades, consider it an early warning sign that he may be heading toward problems with handling peer pressure at some time as he grows up, either because of circumstances in his life or his personality that may make him susceptible. *Does your child appear too timid or too excitable when before he was not? Have circumstances at home changed dramatically for any reason? Is your child suddenly showing extreme sensitivity to what he sees as the group's standards?*

In the next section we'll look at some ways for you to avoid the predicaments we've just summarized. It is much easier to help your child feel strong and secure, which helps him cope with peer pressure than to attempt a Band-Aid solution to the problem after it surfaces.

Part III
How to Help
Your Child Avoid
Peer Pressure
Problems

This section provides you with some suggestions of how to prevent your child from being troubled by peer pressure. Addressing peer pressure problems *before* they happen is preferable to dealing with full-blown problems later. We have also included advice on how to handle the situation if your child is already troubled by having to cope with too much pressure from his friends.

As we have seen in Parts One and Two, the factors that may cause a child to become open to too much influence from peers are primarily tied to circumstances in the home, including lack of supervision, divorce, single parenting, and two-income working families; and a variety of social pressures that our children feel more intensely than might have been the case years ago. It's important to stress again that peer pressure problems are not something that just happen in your child's life; they are usually problems for which causes have been present for some time. This means that you can take steps to prevent real problems from developing by helping out at an earlier stage. Although you may not—and probably will not—be able to control everything about the social environments in which your child lives, by being aware of potential aspects of the home and family that might put the child at risk you can teach him how to react to his peers.

It is the goal of all parents to raise healthy, competent children who will grow into well-functioning adults. This does not happen solely as a result of good intentions, however, as we saw in the case of Jennifer, whose responsible parents were actually hurting her because of their expectations of her. Although we parents would like to believe our children's world meshes with our beliefs, the truth is that the pressures and influences our children face may be experienced by them differently than we imagine. You must understand this, try to see your child's point of view, and take steps to make the child's home life as stable and nurturing as possible.

It is important for you to keep in mind, however, that it is a normal and constructive part of growing up for your child to need acceptance by his peers and that the desire to find companionship, comfort, and security within a group is, in fact, a very strong human need that stays with us throughout our lives. Your goal is not to teach your child to be aloof or indifferent to other children, but to teach him how to deal positively with his peers early on so that friendship will enhance growing up.

ASSESS YOUR FAMILY'S ABILITY TO COPE WITH PEER PRESSURE: PARENTS AS ROLE MODELS

As parents, there are a number of aspects of your own and your family's life that you can evaluate to aid in understanding where you might find problems with your child in dealing with peer pressure. Once you have identified these, you can apply certain strategies to bypass potential difficulties that might put your child at risk.

A helpful first step is to look at yourself in your role as a parent. You probably agree that it's important that you set a good example for your child. You know that your child learns a great deal by watching you and the way you live. You want your child to grow up with values that you cherish because you know that children need a solid, stable background in childhood to succeed in later life.

However, parents don't necessarily examine and evaluate the ways they want to communicate values to their child. Often we feel comfortable in following our own instincts (which are probably based on our own experiences as children). Family therapists frequently find a large difference between what parents think they are teaching and what the children actually see as their parents' belief. In other words, in your child's eyes there may be differences between what you say and what you do. This is often the case when families are in crisis or under a lot of pressure, as Kevin and Susan's parents were. Perhaps even in the best of family situations, such as Jennifer's, what your child sees and learns from the family is not always what you say you think is important.

Your child sees you in your most unguarded moments and knows your foibles sometimes better than you do. It's a matter of common sense that your child will probably learn more from how you actually handle life and what your values are than from what you *say* about them. Don't underestimate your child's ability to observe you and other adults and don't try to fool him. For more on this subject, consult the companion book *How To Be a Good Role Model for Your Child.*

HELPFUL HINT #1—ACTIONS SPEAK LOUDER THAN WORDS

There are two ways in which you communicate values to your child: first, by telling him what is right and what is wrong; and, second, by behaving the way you expect him to behave in your interaction both with him and with other people around you. None of us, of course, acts perfectly consistently with our ideals. In fact, our stated values are at times only guidelines to help us improve, not a statement of how we really manage to live on a day-to-day basis. We perhaps do our best when we are aware of our own shortcomings and the disparity between what we say and what we do. This awareness shows us where we need to keep trying. As parents, however, we sometimes think we should seem more perfect to our children, so we continue to tell our children categorically what they should or should not do, despite our own failures at consistency.

What parents may fail to understand is that they cannot just tell a child what to do and expect unwavering compliance. You cannot simply say to a child, for example, "It's important for you to do well in school because education is important and it's a competitive world out there, so get on with it." No matter how often you say it, you may not succeed if you neither show that you believe what you say nor help provide the environment in which a child can feel good and be reinforced for his efforts to do well in school. Constant reminders alone may seem to your child more like nagging than helping.

Parents become upset and worried when they feel that their child isn't serious enough about school. They truly may want their child to be a good student, go to a good college, and have a good profession. And they become frustrated when their child may seem unmotivated. In such cases, usually, a child understands what his parents want. A possible source of the child's lack of desire may lie in the values really exhibited by his parents. To inspire your child to learn you may need to establish a household in which the process of learning is enjoyed and respected. You and your spouse might include your child in discussions that are interesting to him at a level he understands. You might also make a point of combining learning and entertainment so that family outings are fun and at the same time intellectually stimulating and informative. A parent who never picks up a book or finds time to take a course or generally shows any interest in learning is not a parent whose spoken values about education are going to be taken seriously by a child.

And so it is in other areas. A father who sits in

front of a TV all weekend, watching football or baseball or whatever, is showing his child that watching sports is what's really enjoyable—not reading books, exploring the environment, learning hobbies, or perhaps actively playing sports himself. Likewise a parent who advises a child about the potential negative effects of alcohol abuse is not going to be terribly convincing if he or she routinely comes home intoxicated or drinks too much at home.

Remember, as simple as it may seem to say it, the way to communicate your values is by living *them as well as by stating them.*

HELPFUL HINT #2—BE AWARE OF WHAT YOU'RE MODELING

As we saw with the individual examples in Part Two, parents are the primary models of behavior and values for their children for many years. Often, however, parents may lose sight of what they are being models for. Life is complicated, and all of us are constantly besieged by demands. But it is important for you to stop every so often and see what you're doing in your own life. Before you criticize your child for being wishy-washy or bowing to the demands of the group, take a look at the way you're living your life and how you're handling your own pressures. Before you charge after your child's peers and lay the blame for his misbehavior at their door, look at your own behavior.

Ask yourself if you have a fair, consistent point of view. Are you sure that you are not doing an adult version of some of the things that you don't like your child to do?

Kevin and Susan's parents had modeled many positive aspects of success for their children, and in turn the children were as hard-working and responsible as their parents. They took their school work seriously just as their parents took their work seriously. They were ambitious and goal-oriented similarly to their parents, and the parents were proud that their children had the same values that they had.

Unintentionally, however, the parents had also shown a preoccupation with material things. Their arguments over finances, their worry over a lowered standard of living, etc., impressed their two children about the importance of money and appearances. They also implied—through the collapse of their marriage—that family relationships are not always nurturing or safe.

Parents cannot be superhuman. Thus it's not always apparent to us at a given time—especially when we're under pressure—that we may be serving as a model for the behavior that is just the opposite of what we would like to see in our children. Certainly Kevin and Susan's parents—like all of us—thought that they, as well as their children, would be strong under fire and face a personal crisis with rational thought and perspective. This was not what happened, however, and the resulting chaos created by the parents overflowed into the children's lives with precisely the negative effects Kevin and Susan's parents wished to avoid. *Although it is easy to say, but fundamentally more difficult to do, parents should routinely step back and examine their own behavior.* We are often too close to it to perceive whether it's right or wrong—or, even more important, how we might improve.

Take the case of Jennifer. We saw that her parents were consistent, exemplary models of honesty, consideration, and compassion. They were good citizens. Unintentionally, however, Jennifer's mother also was a model of avoiding arguments and saying yes when she wanted to say no. She had shown her daughter that nice people avoid direct confrontations with their friends. Jennifer's parents had thus been the models for behavior that, at least in some situations, was not helpful for their child and that put her at risk of undue influence by her friends. Unaware of what they were doing, they were shocked when Jennifer got into trouble.

HELPFUL HINT #3—ASSESS YOUR OWN VULNERABILITY TO PEER PRESSURE

A humorous test of your own vulnerability to peer pressure as a parent is "the birthday party dilemma." It happens early in your child's life.

Assuming parents of four- or five-year-olds have the power to determine the type of birthday party their child will have and that children will enjoy almost any kind of celebration, here is the situation:

Your four-year-old daughter was recently invited to several classmates' birthday parties from preschool. In fact, for each party, her entire class of twenty-three children got invitations.

At the first party a magician entertained everyone with elaborate balloon creations, the birthday cake was from an extremely fancy French bakery, and your child returned with a prize bag full of delightful little gifts. Parents were invited to the second party two weeks later and were served white wine and a light buffet in their own reception that took place during the children's party. The birthday child's parents had hired a party organizer to engage the children in games and story-telling. You observed the entire event in surprise; this wasn't how you remembered it when you were a child. On both occasions the birthday child was swamped with gifts, overexcited, and distracted. All the children ate large quantities of sweets, and your daughter came home feeling mildly sick to her stomach.

Your own child's birthday is next month. Already she is excited and has sent out invitations to her school friends and children in the neighborhood. She is requesting pizza for lunch and a clown to entertain her friends. In addition, she reminds you that most of her friends have received a two-wheel bike on their fifth birthday, and that she would like one also.

Although somewhat prepared for her requests, you're uneasy about the developing picture. Your child's vision and your own vision of the party don't mesh. You have noticed that these birthday parties can be costly occasions that tremendously overstimulate and perhaps spoil the children attending, and you begin to wonder how much more elaborate the parties for each succeeding birthday will have to be. If this is the fifth birthday, you reason, what will be required for the tenth? You rationalize your child's requests (and your own inclination to consider them) by telling yourself that maybe times have changed and that perhaps by denying her wishes you will be unnecessarily penalizing your child. After all, you want her to be popular. You want her to be invited to her friends' birthday parties. Perhaps most of all, you don't want your child or yourself or the other parents and their children to think you are a miserly parent.

This is a fundamental test of "parental" peer pressure. If you really think honestly about this situation—and admit to yourself what your own decision might be if you confronted these circumstances—you will have an indication of how peer pressure regarding your child can work on you.

Let's say, however, that this is your chance to be a role model for your child. How important is the party—to you? Do you go with the flow and do things the way the other mothers did? Or do you want to resist this temptation and come up with something interesting for the celebration but something that is more appropriate for five-year-olds? Perhaps you don't want to invite the entire class. You may believe it's better for children to actively participate in the party rather than be professionally entertained. You may think that spending more than $100 on the party is excessive. After all, the purpose of the birthday is to celebrate another year in your child's life, not to entertain parents or provide gifts for the other children. *Can you explain this to your child?*

The "birthday party" can be an early sign of problems with peer pressure for you and your child. For example, when it was time for Ronald's sixth birthday, he actually decided that he didn't want the party in his own home because he was embarrassed about the house. Ronald's parents were moderately successful but not wealthy. They had been able to provide him with the opportunity of attending a small private school in which there were some extremely wealthy children. Ronald had been to a few very elaborate birthday parties, and when it was time for his birthday he wanted to have it at a relative's house which was bigger and in a more expensive neighborhood. And, in fact, the parents gave in to their child's pressure and held the party in the relative's home, complete with a magician and the reception for the parents.

Although the parents might have felt that they were making a positive decision by sparing their child embarrassment, they were actually setting him up as a potential victim of undue peer pressure. In effect, the parents conspired with the child in saying that it's impossible to have a successful birthday party without going to elaborate expense—not because they necessarily thought that to be true but because other parents seemed to believe that. Because they gave in, Ronald assumed that his parents also wanted this level of show.

In situations like this, if you overtly bow to peer pressure, ostensibly for the good of your child, you are providing a lesson that will affect his developing sense of decision making. In reality, you are actually demonstrating your own lack of strength. By producing an affair as elaborate as the others, you are teaching your child the importance of doing what everyone else does. This is especially so if your child suspects in any way that you disapprove of such an elaborate event but will proceed with it anyway. In these circumstances you are in effect saying to your child that, in order to be liked, you must provide the same type of party the other people did. You are reinforcing the message that compliance is very important.

HELPFUL HINT #4—ASSESS YOUR OWN MOTIVATIONS IN REGARD TO YOUR CHILD

To complete the lessons of the birthday party test, take the time to complete the following exercise. Mark your answers to the questions as true or false.

1. Although I want my child to be interested in learning and to have friends who are good students, I watch TV more than I read, and I probably couldn't find time to attend a lecture or take a course in something that might interest me.
(T) (F)

2. I'd be angry if my child cheated on a test and as an excuse told me that everybody did it, but it is

no secret in my house that I am willing to cheat a little on my income taxes.

(T) (F)

3. Sometimes I have spent more on an item that I like or have gone out of my way to get a particular make or brand of clothes or appliance, but it irks me when my child gets fussy about what brand of clothes or toys he needs to have to be like other kids.

(T) (F)

4. I don't want my child to drink alcohol as a teenager and certainly not to drive under the influence, but I admit I drink regularly myself, and my child has seen that I have driven after having had a couple of drinks. (This question can be applied to drugs, cigarettes, or junk food.)

(T) (F)

5. I don't think it is a good idea for children to see movies that are violent or sexually explicit, but my child sees me watching such movies and has access to our cable TV channels, and I'm not always around to monitor what he watches.

(T) (F)

6. I expect my child to be polite and to control his temper, but at home I sometimes lose my temper or am insulting.

(T) (F)

Although what you've read so far in this section has probably influenced your answers to these questions, the point of the test is to drive home to you that you can seem to be doing all the right things for your child when in reality your behavior is sabotaging your message—and your efforts.

HELPFUL HINT #5—EVALUATE YOUR RELATIONSHIP WITH YOUR CHILD

To continue to guide your child until he is mature enough to make his own decisions and establish healthy relationships, there is no better tool than communication. How better will you be able to realize when he has problems, and how else will you be able to aid your child in solving them? Coupled with this ability to communicate, you must be in close enough contact so that you can be a model and so that you know what pressures your child is experiencing. There are two basic aspects, then, to your relationship with your child. *First* is the mutual ability to *communicate*; and *second* is your *active involvement* with your child.

In evaluating your own capabilities in this area, it may be helpful to consider your reactions to the following suppositions. Check the ones that apply to you.

☐ 1. There have been times when I later found out my child had undergone a disappointment or problem that he did not share with me for more than a day. (A variation on this would be for you to have discovered this in some other way.)

☐ 2. Sometimes when my child has a problem, or I'm concerned, my efforts to start a discussion go nowhere and at times seem to make things worse.

☐ 3. There are times when I have felt my child had something on his mind and I didn't want to push it by bringing it up.

☐ 4. My child has told me, "You never listen" or "You don't understand me" or, conversely, "You're always giving me advice" or "You're always nagging me."

☐ 5. My child spends some amount of time every week alone and unsupervised, and I'm not certain of his activities during that time. I feel uncomfortable with that.

☐ 6. In the past three days I have spent less than two hours a day actually talking to my child or getting involved in some activity with him.

☐ 7. I often become involved in my own significant difficulties that have changed how much attention I'd like to give to my child. For example, I have been so aggravated by work on some days that I just can't listen patiently to what happened at school.

☐ 8. Sometimes my child seems older to me than his years. I thought at his age he'd come to me more with his feelings, concerns, and desires.

☐ 9. In the last week there have been times when I haven't known exactly where my child was or what my child was doing.

☐ 10. I would have trouble naming my child's three best friends.

☐ 11. There are times when I really can't understand my child's reactions.

In going through this list, each item you checked may relate to a problem in either communication or active involvement and supervision. However, the fact that you answered yes to one or more of the above questions should not cause you undue concern. There are predictable extenuating circumstances in people's lives at any given time that will influence their answers to any of these fundamental questions about communication and contact. The items are not to be thought of as absolute, but, we hope, will stimulate your thinking about your relationship with your child.

Regarding checkpoint 6, for example, many working fathers and mothers may be concerned that they will not be able to answer yes. If so, it may suggest that although you may not have had time for specific organized activity with your child, other circumstances do exist in the routine of family life that you might want to take advantage of to increase communication. You can share time together over breakfast, for example, or you can speak to each other while simply doing routine things together such as washing the car or cleaning up after a meal. Turning off the TV more often and spending more time talking with each other is an important step in building communication. There is no way to assure continued contact and communication. However, all parents must make a real effort to devote some time to being with their children. Many parents have developed a full range of excuses for why it's difficult to do so—dinner meetings, business travel, gym, aerobics. They might want to consider their motivations behind establishing such a schedule, and they should also assess such a schedule's effects on their children. Probably most important, they should evaluate what they think is the importance of spending time with their children. Research has also shown, furthermore, that it is not just working parents who have time difficulties; more affluent families and families with a parent who does not work outside of the home are also spending less time with their children.

Checking point 6, therefore, does not suggest that you are intentionally uninvolved with your child. It may just be that you are among a large number of parents who have failed to come to terms with the fact that much of their spare time will have to be devoted to family life—especially when their children are small. It's not a popular notion, but it is in fact where a number of well-intentioned parents have gone wrong and have created problems. They just haven't arranged for sufficient contact with their children. Lack of time with your child weakens the parent-child bond and pushes him into earlier associations with friends that may or may not be beneficial to him.

All other things being equal, it is probably true that the less time you spend with your child, the less influence you will be able to exert.

Clearly, we all need to relate to and identify with other people. That's one of the underlying issues that make children reach out to their friends. But if you want to maintain contact with your child, you should realize that you stand the risk of "losing" him to his peer group if you don't spend consistent time with him. If, for example, your child has been pretty much left to his own devices since the age of eight, by the time he reaches fifteen it will be very hard to turn the situation around because your child has already learned to cope with your absence and may prefer that kind of independence. Such a child will have already learned to protect himself from the disappointment of your not being available, and he will have found ways to spend his days that don't include you. Seven years of practice is a long time.

HELPFUL HINT #6—OBSERVE YOUR CHILD

Observing your child is crucial, and a teacher's feedback in this area can also be very helpful. You are well advised, even if no problems seem to exist, to talk with your child's teacher. It's not necessary for your child's teacher to have defined problems for you to benefit from the teachers' knowledge of seeing your child many hours in the day. The teacher has the opportunity to observe his interaction with other children in a way that you may not have the chance to do, and will be more aware of what the normal behavior patterns are for your child's age group.

Arrange a meeting with your child's teacher (or teachers) and ask specifically for impressions of your child. Attempt to find out what kind of potential challenges and developmental issues lie ahead: What does the teacher think you should be looking for? You can start in an open-ended way by obtaining the teacher's initial impressions. Then, if you have specific questions, ask, for example, "Do you think my child is too shy? Does he have trouble speaking up in class?"

Also, you can share with the teacher your own experiences with your child. For example, if you feel that your child tends to be very impulsive, mention that and see if the teacher agrees with you. Find out how the teacher compares your child with the others in his class. Teachers are in a wonderful position to give you valuable impressions, not only because of the amount of time they spend with your child but also because they can provide comparisons with other children of the same age.

Obtaining feedback from teachers can be particularly valuable for parents who have their first child in school or for parents who both work and have limited contact with their child. (Many times parents will first turn to their pediatrician if they have concerns about their child's development; however, pediatricians usually don't see your child often enough, and the doctor's office is not the child's usual social situation.)

It's also a good idea to observe your child when he's with other children of his age group—perhaps at a party or when other children come into the home. How does he interact? Does he seem happy and confident in his relationships? You may see early tendencies that with a little support and guidance you can alter.

If after he completes first or second grade, you find that your child has few or no friends, or he consistently has problems in developing friendships with children his own age, then you could be facing a problem. Usually, children who are not able to interact with others of their own age are insecure and do not think very highly of themselves. High self-esteem and a good sense of self-worth are necessary for later healthy independence. Some conversation with your child to understand his perception of the problem would be a good start. This may lead you to seek ways to help. For instance, if you find your child is too timid to invite friends to the house, you could help him practice an invitation and encourage him to try. You might even make the first invitation yourself. If your child reports that he ends up fighting with other children who don't want to play with him anymore, you would have a different task. Perhaps he needs to find better solutions to everyday conflicts children have when they play. If you are unable to make progress yourself, professional help could be advised. It is far better to consult a therapist and get a clean bill of health than to procrastinate and have a deep-rooted problem on your hands.

HELPFUL HINT #7—HELP YOUR CHILD DEVELOP SKILLS TO BE INDEPENDENT OF PEER GROUP PRESSURES

The following skills are important for all children because they provide good tools. They are discussed below in relation to the type of child who needs the particular skill. The ways parents can help their children develop these skills are also discussed.

The Unassertive Child

Teaching the Unassertive Child to Say No

Being able to say no is an important skill for all children to learn. Being too unassertive to resist peer pressure, as Jennifer was, can become even more of a liability as the child gets older. Pressure to take a drink, to take drugs with friends who are under the influence, or to experiment with sex will confront almost all children at some point before mid-adolescence. It's important for your child to feel confident; when he doesn't want to go along just because everyone is doing it, he must have the self-confidence to be able to either avoid or refuse situations that bother him.

The first step toward helping your child become more assertive is practicing eye contact with him. Eye contact is an important part of asserting oneself, and it may be a special problem for the unassertive child. It's a skill that's easily practiced, however. Explain to your child that people like being looked in the eye and explain that people pay more attention to you when you look them in the eye and that they listen more carefully.

Second, once your child is able to maintain eye contact, practice a confrontation dialogue. Turn it into a game, too. For example, you can play the role of a friend who wants to borrow your child's homework to copy, and your child doesn't want to give it to him. You can then practice showing him how to say no and how to explain to his friend why he can't give him the homework. This also gives you the chance to talk with your child about why people are afraid to say no. You might explain that some people are afraid to get into an argument, either because of a fear that people won't like them anymore or because it has simply become their habit to always go along with what other people want.

In practicing this confrontation dialogue, you might want to have your child act the role of the friend who wants your homework. He might say, for example, "Oh, gee, I didn't have time to do my homework. You wouldn't mind if I just looked at your answers and copied them down real fast before we go into class, would you?" As the parent who wants to be a model for how to refuse the request, you might answer, "No, I'm not really comfortable with that. Sorry." Then reverse the roles so your child can practice saying no.

Start out easily, but keep repeating the exercise. Gradually adopt a more aggressive role so your child can become comfortable with any level of pressure from another child and with different ways to say no. Construct other situations in which a friend might say, "Well, I did you a favor last week. I won't ask you again" or, "Please, please, please. I'm going to get in so much trouble." You want to teach your child the ability to keep saying, "No, I already told you I don't want to do that. And don't ask me again."

The underlying principle to get across is that it's all right to say no. Your child needs to understand that in any relationship you sometimes just have to refuse to do or say or give the other person what he wants. The child must realize that the ability to tell someone how he's feeling is important. If your child doesn't learn this basic skill, then he will feel he must go along with whatever he's asked, no matter how he feels about the situation. The ability to say no provides one cornerstone of your child's social development, and it should be learned before he encounters the major problems that are likely to surface as he grows—alcohol, drugs, driving too fast. Your goal is that he will have learned how to be comfortable in negotiating with other people, that saying no *doesn't* spoil friendships, and it often makes things easier because it solves problems. (It also limits others' aggressiveness because the child is not doing things he doesn't want to do.) Your child will discover that saying no will discourage other children who try to take advantage of him.

Teaching the Unassertive Child to Get What He Wants

There are also times when your child has to be able to assert in a positive manner what he wants. It's the other side of being able to say no. People have labeled it *knowing your bottom line*. It means that your child is able to think through a situation, decide what it is he wants or is willing to do, and stick to it.

For instance, let's say your child is out playing with friends, and you've told him that he needs to call you at six o'clock to let you know where he is. Everyone is having a great time playing a game in which every player is involved. If your child stops to make the phone call, it means that it will disrupt what everyone is doing. Nonetheless, your child needs to be able to say, "I really need to stop for a few minutes right now. It's six o'clock, and I need to make a phone call." That's the child's bottom line. To do so, the child must be prepared to deal with his friends, who might say, "Oh, come on, what's the problem? Just a few more minutes. It will ruin everything."

In this situation you can role-play with your child, just as you did to teach him to say no, to help your child learn to say, "I need to go right now"—and then to go do it. When you begin, you model the assertive behavior first, while your child says the things other children might say to him. Then switch parts and let your child practice his response. Teach him one consistent response that he can follow by making his phone call.

Teach your child that he doesn't have to sit and wait until everyone's happy with his response. It's been shown that assertive children are popular children who can withstand the immediate pressure and displeasure from their friends when they make their needs know.

The Impulsive Child

It takes all children years before they are capable of consistently using good judgment and controlling their impulses. Some children, such as Eric, develop more slowly in this regard. These children require that the structure of their lives be established for them. Here we're discussing a child who needs supervision, who has to be in a predictable situation in which the rules are clear. The impulsive child requires a great deal of stability and consistency. He will do best in situations that won't overstimulate him and put him out of control. This type of energetic child should be taught ways to channel energy in a constructive manner.

Such children, when left to free play on the playground, may get too wound up, but if they're in a structured after-school program with organized games, they'll do much better. They may become so excited when they have friends around that they actually have arguments or end up breaking things. So, when the impulsive child has visitors, parents should make sure that the children have structured activities—because impulsive children usually have trouble organizing themselves. Because of the tendency to become disorganized and wild, parents should take time to help plan activities, whether at home or elsewhere.

Parents should always give such a child clear messages. Most of all, they should not laugh at the child's antics. They shouldn't say, "Oh, he's just being a boy. It's really OK—he'll grow out of it." This may result in the child's continuing to act like he can't control his impulses because he may be confused by your apparent approval of his behavior.

It's very important to be consistent in dealing with this type of child. It is not easy because the child is capable of varying his behavior and may test the rules repeatedly. Only if his parents are consistent and steady will the child be able to gradually change his style. In the meantime, structure and supervision will prevent him from feeling like a "bad kid."

It's often frustrating for parents to deal with a child who is impulsive because he can be exhausting and demanding, especially if you haven't set up clear rules of behavior that help him play constructively. You might want to look at the kinds of toys and movies you provide; perhaps your child needs activities that are more calming. Unfortunately, many parents with impulsive children buy them toys such as swords and guns, which encourage wild, out-of-control play and can even become destructive. Encourage your child to try things to develop his attention span and self-control such as board games, reading, or drawing. When he is involved in more active play, choices that do not encourage aggression are preferable. Body contact sports are extremely arousing to excitable children, and sports such as tennis and swimming are more desirable.

It's extremely important to teach such a child how he can control his own behavior so that he can come to say to himself, "Now, I really should slow down here." In doing this, it's essential that he understand the logical consequences of his actions. Teach him to stop and ask himself, "What will happen if I do this?"

Unfortunately, such internal control of his actions isn't going to come naturally. But you can help teach your child by saying, for example, "When you don't slow down, you get in trouble. Let's think of some ways you can catch yourself before you get so wound up." You can also make a game out of it: "Why don't we see what happens if you say to yourself, 'I need to slow down'?" When you see that your child is learning how to do this, reward him for it by providing affection or a treat. Or you can reward the child for telling you the consequences of a behavior: "What do you think will happen if you do . . . ?" Encourage him to think the situation through. It's a long-term approach, but it works. And because children do want to be good and win approval, the process can be a rewarding one for parents who approach it in the right way.

Sometimes children who are impulsive and have extra energy end up having trouble in early elementary school. It's often hard for them to sit still, pay attention, and adjust to the demands of the classroom. Often, a boy like this is thought of as the class clown. He finds it rewarding to act up because all the kids laugh. Again, unfortunately this will eventually cause the child difficulties with self-esteem. Although the idea of making people laugh may be fun for a while, nobody wants to be thought of as a clown for his entire life, especially as the child gets older and the issues become more serious. An additional problem for impulsive children is that they eventually start to think of themselves as bad. They see themselves as failures, and often anxiety causes more impulsiveness. If you see that happening, you'll want to work with your child on feeling better about himself. Provide gentle understanding about the need to slow down and continually remind him that he's a good person. You will do best if you take a loving, but firm, stand.

Children become more impulsive and unstable

when they are fatigued. If your child already struggles with loss of control problems, it's wise to plan activities that are within the limits of his fatigue.

The Peer Group

So far in this section, we have focused primarily on your child's reaction to the need for social acceptance. We've looked at the factors *inside* your child. But you must also evaluate the child's peer group itself. This in fact can be a major issue: Is the peer group really a problem? Are there times when your own positive modeling, your good relationship with your child, and your help may not be enough? The answer is probably yes. If it's a significant enough problem, you may want to take action regarding the peer group itself.

No matter how you've tried to prepare your child for being a teenager, peer group pressures become more serious in junior high and especially high school. Alcohol and drug abuse at some schools is widespread. For boys in competitive athletics drinking has been reported to be virtually unavoidable by high school age. In fact, substance abuse seems to be part of the sports image highlighted by all the media publicity we see concerning professional athletes who have drug problems. Richard, who is too common an example, was a star on his school football team. His fellow players made it clear that the team played together and partied together and that if he didn't want to drink after a game, he was just not going to make it as a member of the team. He told his mother, "All the guys drink after the game." Those types of pressures are very difficult for a child to resist. In this situation, even a self-confident, popular child is under tremendous pressure from the group, and the thing that makes it so difficult is that the child wants to be a member of the team—it's very important to him. You need to be aware of this pressure. In most cases both the parent and child want the youngster to be active and part of the athletic program. You should realize that the child is susceptible to alcohol and drug use as a member of the team if most of the other players are doing the same thing.

We recommend that you sit down and talk to your child about the possibility that he will be invited to do things that are not appropriate for him and that, in fact, are likely to damage his academic performance and physical well-being. From there you must decide if it's realistic for you to believe he will be able to abstain. If not, you must decide how to approach what will probably be his teenage drinking or drug use.

Another example of peer pressure in high school is reflected in the high rate of teenage pregnancies. Certainly if your daughter is about to enter or is in a school where standards for sexual behavior are liberal, then you should expect her to be confronted with difficult choices. It would be wise for you to pause and look at the situation in which your daughter is likely to find herself. What are the other girls doing? Look at the worst-case scenarios—what kind of behavior is seen as the school standard? Don't rationalize and say to yourself that there are only isolated cases involving children who have family problems or are just "bad kids." Ask yourself and your daughter or son hard questions about what is going on with the other children. If, after this analysis, you determine that most of the youngsters in the school are sexually active and that their behavior seems to prevail, you would be smart to assume that your child probably is in the same category or may well be in the future.

Ongoing frank and supportive talk is in order. First, be a patient listener. Try to explain why such behavior may be hurtful or detrimental and be sympathetic to the pressure your child is encountering. Before you begin offering advice, your child must feel that you understand the situation and his feelings. It is also important for you to help your child to learn how to avoid circumstances that might force such behavior as well as assertive techniques when avoidance isn't possible.

Even if you determine that, down deep, your child is able to maintain a good sense of values and say no to peer pressure, you should realize that your son or daughter is probably still affected by the group's standards. Children are constantly being forced to choose between being accepted as regular members of the group and saying no to things they know are not right. It is the very rare child with spectacular qualities who can consistently go against group norms and remain happy and popular. He needs your help and support when he encounters such pressures, as well as a sure foundation in family values so he can resist negative demands made by his friends. Parents may wish to consult the companion book *Creating a Good Self-Image in Your Child* for information on open and constructive family communication.

HELPFUL HINT #8—KNOW YOUR CHILD'S PEER GROUP

It's very important to evaluate your child's peer group because it will allow you time to anticipate pressures he may encounter. Prevention is the answer to helping your child cope well with peer pressure. If you think about whom your child will be relating to as he grows up, it will help you both respond to the pressures you expect him to encounter. Who are your child's present and potential friends? What are their values?

First, *you need to be knowledgeable about the children and their activities.* Talking with other parents who have older children is a good idea. They can give you information about what their children have encountered.

Second, you need to know whom *your child identifies with most.* Most kids tend to identify most strongly with children they're in class with all day. Relatively few communities are homogeneous in income and social status and in values and background. For most families, schools and communities are very mixed.

If you act early, you can prepare him with a constructive response for pressure he might feel later on. You can teach him alternatives to simply saying yes so he can get along socially. If your child is an athlete, for example, you might expect that he will be faced with the kinds of pressures Richard was, so you should emphasize a message about the need for athletes to be healthy and avoid drinking and smoking. You may also want to become active in school to try to change students' attitudes about drinking. If you know that the standards for sexual behavior in the junior high your child will be attending are loose, you will want to start early in helping both your son and daughter feel secure in family values about casual sex. This requires frank and open communication, which is a process that should be implemented early in your child's life. Your goal is that he come to you to discuss his problems rather than give in to his friends.

After consideration of the school, the children with whom your child will be interacting, and the standards of behavior that will be expected of your child, you may decide you want to change the directions you have already set.

As we said at the beginning, it's a normal human response to be changed by our peers, and no one, especially children and adolescents, can be expected to behave entirely independent of group standards. The pull to conform is powerful. In situations in which a peer group *uniformly* holds particular values and promotes specific behaviors, it may be necessary to remove your child from that group if you do not approve of those values and behaviors. Your child may not be failing you if he accepts the group's standards. He may simply be making choices you would find difficult to resist yourself in the same circumstances. Changing schools or neighborhoods does not always constitute running away from problems. There are certainly times when social environments may be so powerful and negative that removing your child is the only way to protect him.

You can prepare your child to make healthy choices by offering a supportive and involved home-life, by maintaining open communication, and by identifying and dealing with problems early in his development. Finally, you can anticipate peer problems by realistically evaluating the groups in which your child will mature and deciding the degree to which he or any child could remain unaffected. With parental guidance your child will find this peer group to be a source of learning and support on his way to and throughout adulthood.

CONCLUSION

R emember that you are a prime source of help and guidance for your child. If you do your job, your child will grow to be independent and capable and will enjoy and benefit from peers.

Keep your head, a sense of humor, and a sure sense of yourself. That's the best way to help your child with any of the difficult problems he may face on the road to being an adult.

If you think your child may need professional help, it is probably best if you consult a facility that deals with child-family problems. Look for people with training and experience in helping families. Don't accept treatment unless it involves you as the parent. By all means, if your child is doing poorly academically, see someone who can competently rule out the presence of underlying learning disabilities or attention problems. This may involve psychological and educational testing. (For a more complete discussion of what you might expect from therapy, you may wish to consult a companion book in this series, *When Your Child Grows Up Too Fast.*)

REFERENCES

Despert, J. Louise. *Children of Divorce.* Garden City: Dolphin Books, 1962.

Elkind, David. *Hurried Child, Growing Up Too Fast and Too Soon.* Reading, MA: Addison-Wesley, 1981.

Smith, Manuel J. *When I Say No I Feel Guilty.* New York: Dial Press, 1975.

Winn, Marie. *Children Without Childhood.* New York: Pantheon Books, 1983.